HOLY SPIRIT

meditations for the millennium

W9-BIX-698

HOLY SPIRIT
meditations for the millennium

MARK LINK

ThomasMore®
– An RCL Company –

ALLEN, TEXAS

IMPRIMI POTEST
Bradley M. Schaeffer, S.J.

NIHIL OBSTAT
Rev. Msgr. Glenn D. Gardner, J.C.D.
Censor Librorum

IMPRIMATUR
† Most Rev. Charles V. Grahmann
Bishop of Dallas

September 23, 1997

The Nihil Obstat and Imprimatur are official declarations
that the material reviewed is free of doctrinal or moral
error. No implication is contained therein that those
granting the Nihil Obstat and Imprimatur agree with the
contents, opinions, or statements expressed.

ACKNOWLEDGMENT
Unless otherwise noted, all Scripture quotations are
from Today's English Version text. Copyright © American
Bible Society 1966, 1971, 1976, 1992. Used by permission.

Cover photo: Photodisc

Meditations for the Millennium: Holy Spirit is adapted from
Spirit Beyond 2000.

Send all inquiries to:

Thomas More®
An RCL Company
200 East Bethany Drive
Allen, Texas 75002-3804

Toll Free   800–264–0368
Fax   800–688–8356

Vision 2000 on Internet—http://v2000.org

Printed in the United States of America

7422   ISBN 0–88347–422–0

Library of Congress Catalog Card Number: 98–60985

1 2 3 4 5   02 01 00 99 98

Contents

WEEK 1 Virtue of Faith   8

WEEK 2 Virtue of Hope   16

WEEK 3 Virtue of Charity   24

WEEK 4 Gift of Fear of the Lord   32

WEEK 5 Gift of Piety   40

WEEK 6 Gift of Knowledge   48

WEEK 7 Gift of Fortitude   56

WEEK 8 Gift of Counsel   64

WEEK 9 Gift of Understanding   72

WEEK 10 Gift of Wisdom   80

WEEK 11 Fruit of Love   88

WEEK 12 Fruit of Joy   96

WEEK 13 Fruit of Peace   104

WEEK 14 Fruit of Patience   112

WEEK 15 Fruit of Kindness   120

WEEK 16 Fruit of Generosity   128

WEEK 17 Fruit of Faithfulness   136

WEEK 18 Fruit of Gentleness   144

WEEK 19 Fruit of Self-Control   152

Jesus promises the Holy Spirit

Toward the end of his earthly life,
Jesus told his followers, "I shall not
be with you very much longer. . . .
You cannot follow me now . . .
but later you will follow me." John 13:33, 36
Then Jesus added:

"I will ask the Father,
and he will give you another Helper. . . .
He is the Spirit,
who reveals the truth about God. . . .
I will send him to you from the Father . . .

"I have much more to tell you,
but now it would be too much for you
to bear. When, however, the Spirit comes . . .
he will lead you into all the truth."
John 14:16–17, 15:26, 16:12–13

Finally, just before ascending to heaven,
Jesus instructed his disciples,
"Wait for the gift I told you about,
the gift my Father promised . . .
the Holy Spirit." Acts 1:4–5

The Holy Spirit comes

When the day of Pentecost came,
all the believers were gathered together
in one place.

Suddenly there was a noise . . .
like a strong wind blowing,

and it filled the whole house
where they were sitting.
Then they saw what looked like
tongues of fire which spread out
and touched each person there.
They were all filled with the Holy Spirit.
Acts 2:1–4

Later, Peter explained the Pentecost events
to the people of Jerusalem.
He concluded:

"Each one of you must turn away
from your sins and be baptized
in the name of Jesus Christ,
so that your sins will be forgiven; and you
will receive God's gift, the Holy Spirit." . . .

Many of them believed his message
and were baptized,
and about three thousand people
were added to the group that day.
Acts 2:38, 41

The Holy Spirit acts today

Since the first Pentecost,
every Christian who has turned from sin
has received the Spirit in baptism.
Commenting on this, Saint Paul says:

God poured out the Holy Spirit
abundantly on us
through Jesus Christ our Savior,
so that by his grace

we might be put right with God
and come into possession of
the eternal life we hope for. Titus 3:6–7

And since the first Pentecost,
every baptized Christian
has experienced the touch of the Spirit
at special graced moments in their lives.
They may have experienced such a moment
while walking alone on a deserted beach,
or while praying in a church.
They may even have experienced it
while watching a ball game or a movie.

The Holy Spirit touches us in different ways

Christian tradition
describes the activity of the Holy Spirit
in our lives according to three virtues:
faith, hope, and charity (1 Corinthians 13:13),
and seven gifts: wisdom, understanding,
counsel, fortitude, knowledge, piety,
and fear of the Lord (Isaiah 11:1–2).

Tradition also teaches
that when we live in harmony
with the virtues and the gifts of the Spirit,
we are blessed with a variety of "fruits."
In other words, we experience "love, joy,
peace, patience, kindness, generosity,
faithfulness, gentleness, and self-control."
Galatians 5:22–23 (NRSV)

These "fruits" of the Spirit
act as a kind of earthly preview
of the harmony and joy
that will characterize our heavenly life.

The word *fruits* recalls Jesus' image
in John's Gospel, when he says:
"I chose you and appointed you
to go and bear much fruit,
the kind of fruit that endures." John 15:16

And so for the sake of simplicity
and practicality we have structured
Meditations for the Millennium: Holy Spirit
according to the traditional categories of
virtues, gifts,
and fruits of the Spirit.
We begin our spiritual journey, praying:

Breathe into me, Holy Spirit,
that my thoughts may all be holy.
Draw me, Holy Spirit,
that I may love only what is holy.
Strengthen me, Holy Spirit,
that I may defend all that is holy.
Protect me, Holy Spirit,
that I may always be holy.
Saint Augustine

7

Virtue of Faith

A woman was hiking in the Swiss Alps.
Suddenly she was overwhelmed
by the beauty everywhere. She says,
"The throb of emotion was so violent
that I sat down, unable to stand.
Tears filled my eyes, and I thanked God
for creating such a beautiful world."
Later, the thought came to her
that as a poem reflects its poet,
and as a painting reflects its painter,
so creation reflects its creator.
In this sense, the cosmos is a "word"
spoken by God to us. As Scripture says,
"In the beginning . . . God commanded,
'Let there be light'—and light appeared."
Genesis 1:1, 3

Eons later, God spoke a "second word"
to us: the "inspired word" of Scripture.
Much like God's "first word,"
this "second word" was communicated
more through action than through speech.

God guided the Israelites out of Egypt.
God taught them through war and peace.
In short, God didn't merely say, "I love you,"
but showed it in action.

Finally, in the fullness of time,
God spoke a "third word" to us—
the most remarkable word of all.

God spoke through his Son.
Jesus is the "incarnate word" of God,
the word of God "made flesh."

The Letter to the Hebrews
comments on God's "third word" this way:

In the past
God spoke to our ancestors many times
and in many ways through the prophets,
but in these last days
he has spoken to us through his Son.
Hebrews 1:1–2

This brings us to this week's meditations
They focus on the virtue of faith
Faith is the first gift of the Holy Spirit
to our world.

The virtue of faith
is the gift of the Spirit that empowers us
to receive and to embrace
God's revelation to us.

In brief, that revelation comes to us
through these "three words":

- the cosmic word (creation),
- the inspired word (Scripture), and
- the incarnate word (Jesus).

We are now ready to begin our meditations on
the Holy Spirit and the virtue of faith.

Faith is believing
the undreamable dream

To have faith
is to be sure of the things we hope for,
to be certain of the things we cannot see.
Hebrews 11:1

Tennessee Williams wrote a play
called *The Night of the Iguana.*
In a dramatic scene,
Hannah Jelkes says to a man who seems
to have an alcohol problem,
"Liquor's not your problem, Mr. Shannon."
"So what is it?" asks Mr. Shannon.
Hannah says, "The oldest problem
in all the world—the need to believe."

"Faith is the eye that sees Him, the hand
that clings to Him, the receiving power
that appropriates Him." Frederick J. Woodbridge
Which of these is most difficult for me?
What do I believe about Jesus?

The content of Christian faith for Paul
was that Jesus is the Christ (Messiah),
Lord, Son of God,
that He died and through His death
delivered us from our sins and
was raised from the dead
and through His resurrection
communicates new life to those
who believe in him and are baptized.
John L. McKenzie, *Dictionary of the Bible*

Journal

Faith is longing
for something more

[A woman came up behind Jesus.]
She said to herself,
"If only I touch his cloak, I will get well."
Jesus turned around and saw her,
and said, "Courage, my daughter! . . ."
At that very moment
the woman became well. Matthew 9:21–22

Before her conversion and
her remarkable work among the poor,
Dorothy Day spent many a night
in New York's bars.
On her way home around sunrise,
she would often stop in at Mass
at St. Joseph's on Sixth Avenue.
What drew her were the people there
kneeling in prayer. She writes:
"I seemed to feel the faith of those
about me and I longed for their faith."
From Union Square to Rome

The stories of the woman in the Gospel
and of Dorothy Day in New York
invite me to review my own faith journey.
How did the Spirit draw and direct me?
What was a major milestone along the way?

Our generation is remarkable . . .
for the number of people
who must believe in something
but do not know what. Evelyn Underhill

Faith is envisioning a better tomorrow

Journal

Our hope is that God will put us right with him; and this is what we wait for by the power of God's Spirit working through our faith. Galatians 5:5

World War II was in its final days.
President Roosevelt had returned from Yalta,
where he, Churchill, and Stalin
had drawn up the plans for peace.
He had just finished writing a speech
to be delivered the next day—
and was posing for a portrait.
Suddenly he grasped his head
and murmured, "I have a terrible headache!"
Then he slumped forward, unconscious.
A few hours later a stunned nation
got the news: The president was dead.
The last sentence of his undelivered speech
became his final legacy to the nation.
"To all Americans . . . I say:
The only limit to our realization
of tomorrow will be our doubts of today.
Let us move forward
with strong and active faith."

How "strong and active" is my faith
that a better world is possible tomorrow?
What is the basis for my faith?

*Give me faith, Lord,
and let me help others find it.* Leo Tolstoy

Faith is trusting
with all my heart

Your faith . . .
does not rest on human wisdom
but on God's power. 1 Corinthians 2:5

A reporter asked astronaut Ed White
what personal items he took on his Gemini-4
space flight with Jim McDivitt.
He said one precious item was a medal
of Saint Christopher, patron of all travelers.
Pope John XXIII had given a medal to each
astronaut. "I took it on the Gemini-4 flight,"
Ed said, "to express my faith in myself, in Jim
and, especially, in God. Faith," he added,
"was the most important thing
I had going for me on the flight."
Jim McDivitt brought his medal, also, and
hung it on the instrument panel. Ed said,
"Once we were in orbit, and weightless,
it floated on the end of its short chain,
reminding us constantly . . .
of the prayers of our fellow Americans. . . .
It makes you feel very, very small
and humble." *Guideposts Treasury of Faith*

Do I carry any item that expresses my faith?
How do I express my faith in action daily?

Whoso draws nigh to God one step
through doubtings dim,
God will advance a mile
in blazing light to Him. Author unknown

Journal

Faith is pondering the night sky

How clearly the sky reveals God's glory!
Psalms 19:1

When winter invades the South Pole,
total darkness sets in. Richard Byrd
braved four and a half months of this darkness,
alone, to gather weather data.
At times the temperature in his shack
fell to 50 degrees below zero.
To make a long story short, Byrd returned
from the South Pole with something
much more precious than weather data.
His meditations on the rhythm of the stars
and planets circling the night sky
prepared him for the gift of faith.
He wrote in his diary:
"The conviction came to me that the rhythm
was too orderly, too harmonious, too perfect
to be the product of blind chance—
that . . . man was part of that whole
and not an accidental offshoot.
It was a feeling that transcended reason;
that went to the heart of a man's despair
and found it groundless.
The universe was a cosmos, not a chaos."

What does creation say to me about God?

*It takes solitude under the stars
for us to be reminded of our eternal origin
and our destiny.* Archibald Rutledge

Journal

Faith is finding strength in God

*I have the strength
to face all conditions by the power
that Christ gives me.* Philippians 4:13

Bobby Allison, a stock car legend,
compiled an amazing win record.
Then Bobby's fortunes reversed abruptly.
A crash at Pocono International Raceway
ended his career, almost killing him.
A few years later, his youngest son
was killed in the Bush Grand National.
Eleven months later,
his remaining son was killed
in a helicopter crash in Alabama.
Finally, his friend Neil Bonner was killed
just before the 1994 Daytona 500.
Inside Sports magazine
asked Bobby how he was able to accept
the tragedies so calmly and peacefully.
Bobby said, "My faith has helped me,
because I can get down on my knees
and turn to God for strength."

To what extent does my faith help me
to accept tragedies calmly and peacefully?

*With peace in his soul a man can face
the most terrifying experiences.
But without peace in his soul
he cannot manage even as simple a task
as writing a letter.* An English psychiatrist

Faith is frosting
on the windowpane

All we can do is make guesses
about things on earth;
we must struggle
to learn about things that are close to us.
Who, then, can ever hope
to understand heavenly things? Wisdom 9:16

"When I watch a space launch, I am in awe.
It is so far beyond my ability to comprehend.
Television and computers affect me
the same way.
In fact, the marvelous complexity
of my own ear and the eye baffles me.
If I find it hard to fathom these things,
why am I so surprised that I have difficulty
fathoming the things of faith?"
Anonymous

What are some things of faith that I find
hard to fathom? What are some things
in everyday life that I find hard to fathom?

Seeing the immense design of the world—
one image of wonder
mirrored by another image of wonder—
the pattern of fern and feather
echoed by the frost on the windowpane . . .
I ask myself,
"Were those shapes molded by blindness?
Who, then, shall teach me doubt?" Edith Sitwell

15

Virtue of Hope

The Lutheran pastor Dietrich Bonhoeffer
was imprisoned by the Nazis
during World War II.
Just before Christmas 1943, he wrote:

Life in a prison
reminds me a great deal of Advent.
One waits and hopes and putters around.
But in the end
what we do is of little consequence.
The door is shut, and
it can only be opened from the outside.

Bonhoeffer's words could be used
to describe our human situation
before the coming of Jesus and the Spirit.
We were imprisoned by sin.
The door was shut
and we did not have the power to open it.
Then came Jesus and the Holy Spirit.
With them came the gift
of the virtue of hope.

This week's meditations explore this gift.

Perhaps the simplest way
to understand the virtue of hope is to recall
that deep down in every human heart
there is a hunger for eternal happiness.

The virtue of hope
is simply the unshakable trust
that this hunger will be satisfied—
not by our own power,
but by the power of the Holy Spirit.

But we should not think of hope
as something relating only to the future.
On the contrary,
it is something that impacts our lives
in a practical way right now.

It rescues us from discouragement
and sustains us in times of trial.
It fills us with peace and assurance—
even in the midst of turmoil and darkness.

An anonymous poet put it well
when he said:

During the cold, snowy days of winter,
the sun of hope shines in my heart
assuring me
that a spring of flowers is on the way.

Hope is knowing
I have wings

You heard the true message. . . .
You believed in Christ,
and God put his stamp of ownership on you
by giving you the Holy Spirit . . .
the guarantee that we shall receive
what God has promised. Ephesians 1:13–14

Ancient generals put an "ownership stamp,"
such as a tattoo, on their soldiers.
Ancient people put an "ownership stamp"
on their property.
An ancient writer told Christians
to use the image of a dove
(symbol of the Holy Spirit and of hope)
for their "ownership stamp."
Paul likened "ownership stamps"
to God's "gift of the Spirit" to us.
Giving us the Spirit was a sign or
ownership stamp that we belonged to God.

Concretely, in what way—and how clearly—
does God's "ownership stamp" on me
reveal itself to those around me?

Let us be like a bird
for a moment perched
On a frail branch while he sings;
Though he feels it bend,
yet he sings his song,
Knowing that he has wings.
Victor Hugo

Journal

Hope is morning in my heart

May God, the source of hope,
fill you with all joy and peace
by means of your faith in him,
so that your hope will continue to grow
by the power of the Holy Spirit. Romans 15:13

Sir William Mulock retired as chief justice
of Ontario, Canada, in his early 90s.
On his 95th birthday a large group gathered
to honor him. He gave a speech
that touched the hearts of everyone.
A newspaper wrote: "Everyone over 40
should carry that speech in his pocket."
An excerpt from it reads:
"I am still at work, with my hand
to the plow, and my face to the future.
The shadows of evening lengthen about me,
but morning is in my heart. I have . . .
warmed both hands before the fire of life.
The testimony I bear is this: . . .
The rich spoils of memory are mine.
Mine, too, are the precious things of today. . . .
[But the best of all is what lies ahead]
somewhere beyond the hills of time."

What can I do to open myself to the gift
of this kind of hope from the Spirit?

Faith goes up the stairs that love has made
and looks out the windows
that hope has opened. Charles Haddon Spurgeon

Hope is believing in my dreams

Journal

LORD, I put my hope in you. . . .
I have relied on you all my life. Psalms 71:5–6

In 1920 he was hopelessly defeated
as a vice-presidential candidate.
In 1921 he was hopelessly paralyzed,
leaving him with two useless legs.
But Franklin Roosevelt went on to become
the only person in our nation's history
to be elected president for four terms.
During his fourth inaugural address,
he named the person whose spirit of hope
transfused him greatly.
It was Endicott Peabody,
a teacher in his adolescent years.
Peabody once told his students:
"Remember!
Things in life will not run smoothly.
Sometimes we will be rising . . . then,
all will seem to reverse itself . . . [but]
the trend of civilization is forever upward."

Who is one teacher—
or a person other than a parent—
who gave me a transfusion of hope
at a time when I needed it badly? Explain.

The future belongs to those
who believe
in the beauty of their dreams.
Eleanor Roosevelt

Journal

Hope is seeing sunshine through rain

LORD, I put my hope in you; I have trusted in you since I was young. Psalms 71:5

When the Civil War broke out,
Oliver Wendell Holmes volunteered
for the Union and was wounded three times
in three different battles.
After the war,
he graduated from the Harvard Law School,
became a Supreme Court justice in 1902,
and served until his death in 1935.
He said in a speech late in his life:
"As I grow older, I grow calm. . . .
I do not lose my hopes. . . . I think it
probable that civilization will somehow last
as long as I care to look ahead . . . .
I think it not improbable that man,
like the grub that prepares a chamber
for the winged thing it has never seen . . .
may have cosmic destinies
he does not understand."

What tends to keep me from having
the kind of hope Oliver Wendell Holmes had?
What might I do to try to deepen my hope?

Behind the cloud the starlight lurks,
Through showers the sunbeams fall;
For God, who loveth all His works,
Has left His hope for all.
John Greenleaf Whittier

Hope is love pouring
a glass of wine

*The lord is near to those
who are discouraged;
he saves those who have lost all hope.*
Psalms 34:18

People ridiculed Alexander Graham Bell,
dubbing him "the crank who says
he can talk through wire."
He went on to invent the telephone.
People gave up on Helen Keller
when she lost both her sight and her hearing
before the age of two.
She went on to become a famous author
and lecturer.
People wrote off Feodor Dostoevski
when he was sent to a Siberian prison camp.
He survived to become
one of history's greatest novelists.
People said the political career of Abe Lincoln
was over when he was defeated
for public office for the ninth time.
He went on to become
one of history's greatest presidents.

What are two things I hope for, even though
they seem impossible to attain?

*Expect the best!
It lies not in the past.
God ever keeps the good wine till the last.*
William Pierson Merrill

Journal

Hope is taking hold of a helping hand

May our Lord Jesus Christ himself and God our Father, who loved us and in his grace gave us unfailing courage and a firm hope, encourage you and strengthen you to always do and say what is good. 2 Thessalonians 2:16–17

Ben Carson grew up in poverty in Detroit. Worse yet, his father divorced his mother when he was eight.
She made ends meet by working, at times, at three low-paying jobs at one time.
Yet, she found time to encourage him, saying, "You can be anything you want to be. Just ask God. He will help you if you help yourself."
Today, Dr. Carson is one of America's leading pediatric neurosurgeons.
Speaking to high schoolers at his alma mater, he said, "Think big! Set your sights as high as Mount Everest. Nobody was born to be a failure."
Christopher News Notes (Feb. 1993)

What motivates me to keep striving to do what others consider impossible?

Hope is taking hold of a helping hand when the sky turns dark, the wind blows furiously and the road grows steep. Anonymous

Hope is a glimmering taper of light

*The lord is all I have,
and so in him I put my hope.* Lamentations 3:24

From ancient times
South Africa has been plagued
with locust swarms so thick and dense
that they literally block out the sun.
Worse yet, the locusts descend on the crops
and strip them bare. A hard winter follows.
But then a remarkable thing happens.
When fall comes and the locusts die,
their bodies blanket the ground
and act as fertilizer for the new seed.
Result? Next year's crops are bountiful.
Charles Hembree observes:
"This is a parable of our lives.
There are seasons of deep distress
and afflictions that sometimes
eat all the usefulness of our lives away.
Yet, the promise is that God will restore
those 'locust years' if we endure.
We will reap if we faint not." *Fruits of the Spirit*

Why do you think God allows this kind
of pattern to exist in so many lives?

*Hope, like the glimmering taper's light,
Adorns and cheers our way;
And still, as darker grows the night,
Emits a brighter ray.* Oliver Goldsmith

Virtue of Charity

The Pickfords were exchanging gifts
on Christmas. Grandfather Pickford
grew excited as little Peter struggled over
to his chair with a huge box—
obviously wrapped by himself.
The grandfather wrote later:

I carefully unwrapped the box.
I looked inside and said,

"Well, Peter, what a joke you played
on your old grandfather.
You forgot to put anything in the box."

With a startled look, he raised on tiptoes,
looked in the box and then said to me,
"Oh, no, Granddaddy, I didn't give you
an empty present. I filled it with love!"
Letter to "Dear Abby," *Chicago Tribune* (Dec. 22, 1996)

That story makes a good introduction
to the final major gift or "virtue"
that the Holy Spirit bestows on us: charity.
Saint Paul refers to it this way:

God has poured out his love into our hearts
by means of the Holy Spirit. Romans 5:5

Your life must be controlled by love,
just as Christ loved us
and gave his life for us. Ephesians 5:2

The Greek language uses three words
to designate love: *eros, philia,* and *agape.*
Eros usually refers to *sexual* love; *philia,* to
friendship love; and *agape,* to *Christian* love.
Agape empowers us to love God
and one another as Jesus loved us.
Agape is frequently translated into English
by the word *charity.*

This week's meditations focus on *charity.*

In preparation for these meditations,
it might be good to review
the first three gifts that the Holy Spirit
bestowed on us: the virtues ("powers")
of *faith, hope,* and *charity.*

Faith empower us
to receive and to embrace God's revelation
or word (cosmic, inspired, and incarnate).

Hope empower us
to trust that the hunger we experience
for eternal happiness will be satisfied
by the power of the Spirit working in us.

Charity empowers us
to love God and one another with
the same special kind of "Christian" love
with which Jesus loved us.

Love is singing in the morning

Journal

There is nothing in all creation that will ever be able to separate us from the love of God. Romans 8:39

His obituary reads: "J.C. Penney
was one of the few 20th-century merchants
who created a vast financial empire
from virtually nothing."
Penney did the same with his personal life.
In 1929, from a hospital bed, he wrote
farewell letters to his wife and son,
fearing he wouldn't last the night.
Later he wrote, "When I awoke
the next morning I was surprised to find
that I was still alive.
 Going down stairs, I heard singing. . . .
Going into the chapel,
I listened with a weary heart. . . .
Suddenly, something happened. . . .
I felt as if I had been transported
from hell to paradise. I felt the power of God
as I never had felt it before.
I realized that God with his love
was there to help me." The rest is history.

How convinced am I of God's love for me?

As long as anyone has the means of doing good to his neighbor, and does not do so, he shall be reckoned a stranger to the love of the Lord. Saint Irenaeus

Journal

Love is finding a priceless treasure

Jesus said, "No one can see the Kingdom of God without being born again. . . . A person is born physically of human parents, but is born spiritually of the Spirit." John 3:3, 6

The Arabian tale
"Ali Baba and the Forty Thieves"
dates from the 15th century.
One day Ali Baba is hiding in a cave.
Forty thieves appear carrying treasures.
They stop before a great rock. Then the leader
calls out, "Open, Sesame!"
At once, the rock swings open,
revealing a whole sea of stolen treasure.
After the thieves store their new treasure,
their leader calls out, "Shut, Sesame!"
and the rock swings shut again.
Then the group departs.
At this point, Ali Baba goes up to the rock and
utters the magic words: "Open, Sesame!"
The rock obeys, and Ali Baba will never
be poor again. At that moment he is reborn.

The Holy Spirit does for us, spiritually,
what the words did for Ali Baba, materially.

How am I showing my gratitude to God
for this priceless treasure?

*Gratitude to God should be as regular
as our heartbeat.* E. C. McKenzie

Love is possessing
a sacred flower

Journal

Give thanks to the Lord . . .
His love is eternal. Psalms 118:1

At a homily of the Mass at Fatima, Portugal,
on May 13, 1981, Pope John Paul II said
to the million people attending it:
"On this very day last year . . . in Rome,
the attempt on the pope's life was made
in mysterious coincidence
with the anniversary of the first apparition
at Fatima on May 13, 1917.
I seemed to recognize in the coincidence
of the date a special call
to come to this place.
And so today I am here."
After Mass the Holy Father asked Mary,
the mother of Jesus,

to intercede for the world as she did
for the married couple at Cana.
He ended by asking the Spirit for this grace:
"Let there be revealed once more
in the history of the world
the infinite power of merciful love."

How is the infinite power of merciful love
being revealed in my life right now?

Divine love is a sacred flower,
which in early bud is happiness,
and in its full bloom in heaven.
Eleanor Louisa Hervey

27

Journal

Love is having the key to every dream

"I do not call you servants any longer. . . . Instead, I call you friends." John 15:15

Jerome K. Jerome wrote a play called
The Passing of the Third Floor Back.
The plot goes something like this.
A stranger comes to a boarding house
of misfits. These misfits
in some production of the play
wore signs listing their defect:
"cheat," "pimp," "hustler," and so forth.
The stranger's compassion for the misfits
transforms them and the boarding house.
Then one day the stranger
in the "third floor back" passes away.
The rest of the play deals with the misfits
telling how his love changed their lives.

How does the play mirror
the transformation Jesus effected
in the ancient world by his love for us?
How prepared am I to follow Jesus' pattern
of action for changing our modern world?

*There is no difficulty that love
cannot conquer;
No sickness it cannot heal;
No door it cannot open;
No gulf it cannot bridge;
No wall it cannot throw down.*
Emmet Fox (slightly adapted)

Love is being faithful to my calling

*I may be able to speak the languages
of human beings and even of angels,
but if I have no love,
my speech is no more than a noisy gong. . . .
Love is patient and kind;
it is not jealous or conceited or proud;
love is not ill-mannered or . . . irritable;
love does not keep a record of wrongs;
love is not happy with evil,
but is happy with the truth.
Love never gives up. . . . Love is eternal.*
1 Corinthians 13:1, 4–8

Saint Paul's beautiful passage on love
was a favorite of Jefferson, Lincoln,
and Franklin D. Roosevelt.
The famous journalist William Allen White
requested it be read at the funeral services
of his daughter when she was
tragically killed at the age of eighteen.
It has been a guide for life
and a source of comfort to countless people
since it was penned 2,000 years ago.

Which of Paul's descriptions of love
do I find most challenging and why?

*The ancient words of Paul [on love]
have always seemed to me to hold
the complete answer to all human living.*
Novelist Marjorie Rawlings

Journal

Love is fulfilling life's mission

*I may have all knowledge
and understand all secrets . . .
but if I have no love,
this does me no good.* 1 Corinthians 13:2–3

A physician who had been privileged
to share the most profound moments
of people's lives,
including their final moments, said:
"Let me tell you a secret.
People facing death don't think about
what degrees they have earned,
what positions they have held or
how much wealth they have accumulated.
At the end, what really matters—
and is a good measure of a past life—
is who you loved and who loved you.
The circle of love is everything."

Applying the physician's "secret" to my life,
as I am currently living it,
what kind of priority am I placing
on the "circle of love" in my life?

*Each one has a mission to fulfill,
a mission of love. At the hour of death
when we come face to face with God
we are going to be judged on love,
not how much we have done,
but how much love we have put
in the doing.* Mother Teresa of Calcutta

Love is
thinking together

Every husband
must love his wife as himself. Ephesians 5:33

Andy was married to a girl named Kim,
 and things weren't going well.
He consulted a lawyer who had known him
since he was a boy. After explaining
the problem, he asked the lawyer
to prepare separation papers.
The lawyer peered over his classes at Andy,
whom he knew better than Andy thought.
He said, "Andy, don't separate from Kim now.
Wait six months. In the meantime, buy her
flowers regularly; call her from work daily;
take her to dinner every Friday night.
Then go through with the separation.
That'll show her what a mistake she made."
Very, very reluctantly, Andy agreed.
Six months later, the lawyer
ran into him on the street and said,
"Andy, your papers are ready." Andy said,
"I intended to call you. I've decided not to
separate from Kim. You wouldn't believe
how she has changed since I last saw you."
Guess who changed and why?
How can I use the old lawyer's advice
to enrich my own relationships with others?

In marriage, the important thing is not
thinking alike, but together. Anonymous

Gift of Fear of the Lord

The reaction of a squirrel to a child
stooping to offer it a nut is interesting.
The squirrel's front legs strain forward,
attracted by the offer;
its back legs strain backward, fearful of it.

In his book *The Idea of the Holy,*
Rudolf Otto describes our response to God
in a similar paradoxical way.
It is a blend of fear and fascination.

An example of this paradox is the sea.
Poet Rod McKuen says that he loves the sea,
but that doesn't make him less afraid of it.
In other words, the sea's beauty attracts.
But, at the same time, its awesome power
makes us fearful of it.

And so the psalmist says of God,
in almost the same breath:
"I love you, LORD!" Psalms 18:1
But I "serve the LORD with fear." Psalms 2:11

Saint Augustine sees "fear of the Lord"
as the "first step" in the spiritual life.

The prophet Isaiah lists
the seven "gifts of the Spirit" as follows:
wisdom, understanding, counsel, fortitude,
knowledge, piety, and fear of the Lord.

Saint Augustine says of Isaiah's list:

*The prophet begins with wisdom
and ends with fear of the Lord. . . .
He begins, therefore,
by identifying the* goal *we are striving for
and ends with the starting point
where we must begin.*

*Thus, to the question,
"How does one secure wisdom?"
he answers, By your understanding.
And similarly, if we ask,
"How are we to arrive at understanding?"
he answers, By counsel.*

*And "How shall we secure counsel?"
he answers, By fortitude.
"And fortitude?" By knowledge.
"And knowedge?" By piety.
"And piety?" By fear of the Lord.*
Quoted in The Teaching of Saint Augustine
on Prayer and the Contemplative Life by Hugh Pope

So Scripture says, "The fear of the LORD
is the beginning of wisdom." Psalms 111:10 (NRSV)

This week's meditations focus on
the "starting point" of the spiritual life.
It is "fear of the Lord,"
the gift of the Spirit
that draws us away *from* sin *to* God.

Fear of the Lord
is a blessing

If we say that we have not sinned,
we make a liar out of God,
and his word is not in us. 1 John 1:10

A disorder of the nervous system
left a small child with no sense of pain.
One day the mother heard the child
laughing in the next room.
She went in to see what was going on.
The child was chewing on her finger
and amusing herself
by drawing on the wall with the blood.
The loss of a sense of pain
is like the loss of a sense of sin.
It destroys our awareness to the
tragic seriousness of our situation.
The closer we are to God, the more aware
we are of God's holiness and our sinfulness.
The farther we are from God,
the less aware we are of these two things.
In other words, distance from God blurs
the difference between holiness and sin.
If we are far enough away, we may not
even be aware of any difference.

How aware am I of my own sinfulness?

There are only two kinds of people:
saints who see themselves as sinners;
sinners who see themselves as saints.
Anonymous

Journal

Fear of the Lord is respecting creation

When my bones were being formed,
carefully put together
in my mother's womb . . .
you knew that I was there—
you saw me before I was born.
Psalms 139:15–16

A poster on the wall of a post office
in Tulsa informed citizens
that it was a violation of federal law
to kill an eagle.
Moreover, the federal law
extended its protection to eagle eggs—
that is, to unborn eagles.
The Tulsa poster triggered this thought
in author Michael Staton: "Isn't it ironic
that we pass laws to protect unborn birds
but refuse to pass laws
to protect unborn humans?"

How comfortable am I with
our nation's attitude toward human life?

All human life—
from the moment of conception
and through all subsequent stages—
is sacred, because human life is created
in the image and likeness of God.
Nothing surpasses the greatness
or dignity of a human person.
Pope John Paul II

Fear of the Lord
is "flying in Jesus"

*You have changed my sadness
into a joyful dance;
you have taken away my sorrow
and surrounded me with joy.* Psalms 30:11

"Rhythm & blues superstar R. Kelly
joined Kirk Franklin for a concert at the
University of Illinois Chicago Campus
Pavilion. . . . The Chicago singer
walked on stage in a gray suit.
When the cheers died down, Kelly said:
'It's been a long time coming but
here I am. Some may think it's a gimmick
but I tell you, here stands a broken man. . . .
I've come to find out
that whatever it is you want,
it is in the Lord. I used to be flying in sin—
now I'm flying in Jesus.'. . .
Kelly's voice was pained and peeling,
like a Pentecostal sinner now preaching
the light." *Chicago Tribune* (Mar. 8, 1997)

Have I ever wondered why
I've not been overwhelmed by the Spirit,
as some people have been?
What might be one reason?

*The time when I was converted
was when religion became
no longer a mere duty, but a pleasure.*
John L. Lincoln

Journal

Fear of the Lord is being grateful

Jesus said, "Why is this foreigner the only one who came back to give thanks to God?" Luke 17:18

"Our Father in heaven, if ever we had cause to offer unto Thee our fervent thanks, surely it is now, on the eve of our Thanksgiving Day, when we the people of this nation are comfortable, well-fed, well-clad, and blessed with good things beyond our deserving.
May gratitude, the rarest of all virtues, be the spirit of our observance. . . . May the desperate need of the rest of the world, and our glorious heritage, remind us of the God who led our fathers every step of the way by which they advanced to the character of an independent nation. For if we do not have the grace to thank Thee for all that we have and enjoy, how can we have the effrontery to seek Thy further blessings?
God, give us grateful hearts.
For Jesus' sake. Amen "
Peter Marshall, delivered in the U.S. Senate, Nov. 26, 1947

How would I answer the question posed by Peter Marshall in his prayer?

Whoever eats food without giving thanks steals from God. Old Jewish saying

Fear of the Lord
is knowing our fate

*Whoever has the Spirit . . . is able to judge
the value of everything.* 1 Corinthians 2:15

War hero General George Patton
was toppled from his hero's pedestal by
General Eisenhower for reckless remarks
about the war. Appropriately, the movie
Patton ends with the hero commenting
on the fleeting nature of glory.
He describes how the Roman people
welcomed home their victorious generals
with a great parade.
"In the procession came trumpeters . . .
and strange animals from conquered
territories, together with carts laden
with treasures. . . . The conqueror rode
in a triumphal chariot, the dazed prisoners
walking in chains before him. . . .
A slave stood behind the conqueror holding
a golden crown and whispering in his ear
a warning that all glory is fleeting."

What does Patton's closing reflection
say about my priorities and values?

*Movie star Tom Selleck said, "Whenever
I get full of myself, I remember
the elderly couple who approached me
in Honolulu with a camera. When I struck
a pose for them, the man said, 'No, no,
we want you to take our picture!' "*

Journal

Fear of the Lord
is turning back to God

As you were once determined to turn away from God, now turn back and serve him with ten times more determination.

Baruch 4:28

Father Zossima is a character in
Dostoevski's novel *The Brothers Karamazov.*
Zossima's brother, who had left his faith, returns
to it during his last illness.
The novelist says of the brother:
"The first birds of spring
were flitting in the branches, chirping
and singing at the windows. . . . Looking at
them and admiring them, he began suddenly
begging their forgiveness. . . . 'Birds of
heaven, happy birds, forgive me,
for I have sinned against you too.'
None of us
could understand that at the time,
but he shed tears of joy.
'Yes.' he said,
'there was such glory of God all about me;
birds, trees, meadows, sky,
only I lived in shame and dishonored it all
and did not notice the beauty and the glory.'"

How do I interpret the brother's remarks?

*Wisdom is a gift; but, like all gifts,
it can't be forced upon us. We must open
ourselves to receive it.* Anonymous

Fear of the Lord is life-giving

*Reverence for the lord
gives confidence and security.* Proverbs 14:26

When Buckminster Fuller died
at the age of 88, he held 170 patents—
one for an underwater submarine base.
He was best known, however,
as the inventor of the geodesic dome,
capable of spanning 800 feet.
But Fuller's life wasn't always a success.
Glenn Van Ekeren describes a wintry night when
Fuller stood on the snowy shores
of Lake Michigan contemplating suicide.
He was 32, bankrupt, and depressed.
Just before leaping into the frigid waters,
he happened to glance up
into the star-filled night sky.
As he did the thought came to him:
"Do I have the right to end my life?"
The answer was clearly, "No!"
He went on to become an engineer,
an architect, a poet, and a philosopher.

What does Buckminster Fuller's story
say to me?

*Life is raw material. We are artisans.
We sculpt our existence
into something beautiful, or debase it
into ugliness. It is in our hands.*
Cathy Better

39

Gift of Piety

The gift of piety recalls the story
of Saint Patrick of Ireland.
At sixteen, he was captured by pirates.
For six years he was kept as a slave.
During the long hours and days of tending
flocks all alone, he taught himself
to pray and meditate. He says:

I used to stay
in the woods and on the mountain, and
before the dawn I'd be aroused to prayer,
in snow and frost and rain . . .
because then the spirit was fervent within.

The saint is describing the gift of piety.
It is that moment when the Holy Spirit
touches our hearts in a profound way.
Saint John of the Cross says this moment
is the foundation of the spiritual life.
It awakens in us the mystery of God.

This awakening lifts us out of ourselves
and makes us aware of a whole new world.

For example, one evening in his youth,
Bede Griffiths was walking outside alone.
Suddenly he became aware
of the sound of birds singing in chorus.
He said he had never heard birds singing
so beautifully.
As he walked on, he came upon some
hawthorn trees in full bloom.

The sight and the smell were intoxicating.
Finally, just as the sun was setting,
he came to an open field. He writes:

Everything then grew still. . . .
I remember now the feeling
of awe that came over me,
I felt inclined to kneel on the ground. . . .

Now that I look back on it, it seems to me
that it was one of the decisive events
of my life. Up to that time I had lived
the life of a normal schoolboy,
quite content with the world as I found it.

Now I was suddenly made aware
of another world of beauty and mystery. . . .
It was as though I had begun to see
and smell and hear for the first time.
Bede Griffiths, *The Golden String*

All of us have experienced
similar moments like this in our own lives.
They are moments when the Holy Spirit
touches and graces us
at the deepest level of our being.

And so this week's meditations
focus on the gift of piety—
and the various ways it manifests itself
and enriches our life.

Piety is knowing that God is near

[Moses pleaded to see God. God said,]
"When the dazzling light of my presence
passes by, I will . . . cover you
with my hand until I have passed by.
Then I will take my hand away,
and you will see my back but not my face."
Exodus 33:22–23

Karen Karper rarely saw deer near her house
during the day. But at night, she heard them
prowling about and, in the morning, saw
their footprints on her lawn. She writes:
"If you are in the right place
at the right moment, you will see deer,
perhaps even very close at hand.
But once you try to touch them, they flee."
Then she adds:
"[It is the same] with the comings and
goings of the Spirit of God. If I wait quietly
going about the tasks of my day,
I might glimpse a trace of His activity
in my life, a subtle sign that He is
just beyond the edge of my vision."
Where God Begins to Be

Can I recall a time when I glimpsed
a trace of the activity of God's Spirit
in my life? What? How did it affect me?

If I walk one step toward God,
God will run ten steps toward me. Anonymous

Journal

Piety is knowing
Christ lives in me

A voice said from the cloud,
"This is my Son, whom I have chosen—
listen to him!" Luke 9:35

Nathaniel Hawthorne
wrote a story called *The Great Stone Face.*
It concerns a sculpture that an artist
cut into the side of a mountain.
A young boy, named Ernest, was captivated
by the kindness and nobility that
the artist was able to put into the face.
Ernest was also captivated by an old legend
that someday a man would appear who
would bear a great resemblance to the face.
Even after he'd grown to adulthood,
Ernest couldn't help admiring the face,
meditating on it, to be able to recognize
the man spoken of in the legend.
Then one day the man appeared.
The people in Ernest's village exclaimed,
"Behold, behold, Ernest is himself
the likeness of the Great Stone Face."

How might this story serve as a parable
of our Christian vocation?

It is no longer I who live,
but it is Christ who lives in me. . . .
I live by faith in the Son of God,
who loved me and gave his life for me.
Galatians 2:20

Piety is achieving spiritual focus

Turn to the LORD and pray to him,
now that he is near. Isaiah 55:6

Edward Hays tells a story of a disciple
who went to visit a holy man.
When the disciple arrived,
the holy man was sitting statue-still,
completely absorbed in prayer.
Not an eye blinked, not a finger moved,
not a muscle twitched.
When the holy man concluded his praying,
the disciple spoke to him in awe and asked,
"Where did you learn such stillness
and such total concentration?"
The man replied, "From my cat.
She was watching a mouse hole
with even greater concentration
than you observed in me now." *Secular Sanctity*

To remain reverent and focused
in God's presence is true prayer.
Do I ever rest focused in God's presence,
totally open to whatever grace
the Spirit wishes to bless me?

The LORD said,
"I was ready to answer my people's prayers,
but they did not pray.
I was ready for them to find me,
but they did not even try." Isaiah 65:1

Journal

Piety is being touched by the Spirit

Bring pure olive oil . . .
for the lamps in the Tent, so that a light
might be kept burning regularly. Leviticus 24:2

A London theater director challenged
novelist Jill Paton Walsh for criticizing
the religious practice of lighting candles.
Noting that fire is a religious symbol of God
and as old as the Bible itself, he said
that lighting a candle can be a profound
expression of faith.
"To light a candle is an act of poetry
as well as an act of piety."
Then he gave this personal experience
to illustrate the power of ritual.
In a certain play, an actor's role was simply
to kneel on stage saying the rosary.
The actor had ceased practicing his faith.
But night after night, as he knelt on stage,
saying the rosary, he began reflecting
on what he was doing.
Suddenly it became real. He began *praying*
the rosary. At that moment he was touched
deeply by the Spirit. James Roose-Evans,
"Keep the Candles Burning" in *The Tablet* (Mar. 8, 1997)

What is one religious ritual that I perform?
How might I make it more prayerful?

What greater calamity can fall upon a nation
than the loss of worship? Ralph Waldo Emerson

Piety is radiating the Spirit

The people honored Joshua all his life, just as they had honored Moses. Joshua 4:14

Alec Guinness played the British colonel
in *The Bridge on the River Kwai.*
His autobiography, *Blessings in Disguise,*
describes a moving episode
that began to thaw his anti-Catholicism and
prepare the way for his becoming a Catholic.
He was in a film being shot in France.
One night, dressed for his priest's role,
he was walking to the film site.
A small boy ran up, grabbed his hand,
swung it playfully, and prattled on nonstop.
Alec writes: "He obviously took me for
a priest and so to be trusted. Suddenly with
a 'Bon soir, mon pere' . . . he disappeared. . . .
I was left with an odd calm sense of elation.
Continuing my walk, I reflected that a
Church which could inspire such confidence
in a child, making its priests . . . so easily
approachable could not be as scheming
and creepy as so often made out."

What kind of reverence do I have for persons
and things linked to God in a special way?

Shine through me and be so in me
that every soul I come in contact with
may feel your presence in my spirit.
John Henry Newman

Journal

45

Piety is plunging into an inner ocean

*Jesus went . . . to a lonely place,
where he prayed.* Mark 1:35

During the 1978 blizzards in Ohio,
James Truly's tractor-trailer
skidded off the shoulder of the road
and wound up in a deep ditch.
He turned on his CB radio but to no avail.
Since it was 5 A.M. and the snow
was blowing and drifting badly,
he decided to wait for daylight
to go for help.
When Truly woke up a few hours later,
his truck was completely frozen shut
and covered with snow.
He braced himself for a long wait.
It turned out to be six days.
After his rescue, reporters asked Truly,
"How did you spend those six long days?"
He replied, "I did a lot of meditating."

Where do I meditate best? What are some
practical benefits I derive from meditation?

Meditation is not an escape
from daily living, but a preparation for it. . . .
Like pearl divers, meditators plunge deep
into the inner ocean of consciousness
and hope to come swimming back
to the surface with jewels of great price.
Ardis Whitman

Piety is tapping into the power of prayer

*God purposely chose
what the world considers nonsense
in order to shame the wise,
and he chose . . .
what the world looks down on . . .
to destroy
what the world thinks is important.*
1 Corinthians 1:27–28

Young Joseph of Cupertino
labored under a learning disability and
was considered dull and clumsy
When he tried to enter the religious life,
he was turned down
by one monastery after another.
Finally, in spite of his disability,
a Franciscan group agreed to accept him.
Joseph acquired enough knowledge
to be ordained a priest.
Eventually, many miracles were attributed
to him and many credible people,
including Pope Urban VIII,
saw him "levitate" while praying.
His constant admonition to people was
"Pray, pray, pray!"

What is the greatest challenge I face
when it comes to prayer?

*If you are a stranger to prayer,
you are a stranger to power.* Anonymous

Gift of Knowledge

A young man was jogging
along a deserted country road.
Suddenly, he noticed the spectacular colors
of an autumn tree.
He stopped dead in his tracks.

As he stood marveling at the tree's beauty,
he recalled how Edward Dickinson,
father of poet Emily Dickinson, was so
moved by a brilliant display of northern lights
that he rang village church bells
to alert the other villagers
so that they could also enjoy it.

The jogger's experience of the tree
and Edward Dickinson's experience
of the northern lights bring to mind
an observation by Ralph Waldo Emerson.

If stars should appear one night
in a thousand years,
how we would believe and adore
and preserve
for many generations the remembrance.

And this introduces us to
the sixth "gift of the Holy Spirit"—
the gift of knowledge.

We may describe it as
an illumination that empowers us to see
everything as coming from God,

pointing to God, and leading to God.

A concrete example
of the difference this gift makes
is the story of an old Arab.
After hearing a Westerner lecture
on the marvels of a telescope, he said:

You foreigners see millions of star,
but nothing beyond.
We Arabs see only a few stars—and God.

An so the gift of knowledge
empowers us to experience creation
the way the psalmist did:

How clearly the sky reveals God's glory!
How plainly it shows what he has done!
Each day announces it to the following day;
each night repeats it to the next.
No speech or words are used,
no sound is heard, yet their message
goes out to all the world and is heard
to the ends of the earth. Psalms 19:1–4

It is to the gift of knowledge
that we now turn.

Knowledge is seeing as the Spirit sees

God is the only . . . judge. . . .
Who do you think you are,
to judge someone else? James 4:12

A king had four wonderful sons.
But each had the same problem.
Possibly because of their royal status,
they felt their judgment of people and
of situations was always the right one.
And so one wintry day
the king told his eldest son
to ride out to a grove of fruit trees and
write a brief description of what he saw.
Secretly, the king had his other sons
do the same thing: one going in spring,
one in summer, and the other in fall.
Then the king called his sons together
and asked each to read to the others
his description.
The first called it "barren and depressing."
The second called it "a cloud of green buds."
The third called it "a sanctuary for birds."
The fourth called it "a paradise of fruit."

How might the king's lesson to his sons
apply to my life right now?

Don't judge others by what they say
about something or someone;
try and find out
what makes them say it. Anonymous

Journal

Knowledge is proof of the Spirit

*My teaching and message
were not delivered with skillful words . . .
but with convincing proof
of the power of God's Spirit.* 1 Corinthians 2:4

TV celebrity Malcolm Muggeridge
interviewed Mother Teresa of Calcutta.
The verdict of the videotaped interview
was that it was hardly usable.
Mother Teresa's delivery was halting
and her accent was thick.
One BBC official, however,
felt that the interview had a mysterious power
and decided to air it on a Sunday night.
Response to the program was amazing—
both in terms of mail and contributions.
What came through was not "skillful words"
but "the power of God's Spirit"
speaking through Mother Teresa—
the same power that Paul talks about
in today's Bible reading.

Can I recall a time
when the Spirit seemed to strengthen
or guide me in some situation?

*As the earth can produce nothing
without the energizing power of the sun,
so we can do nothing
without the energizing power of the Spirit.*
Anonymous

Knowledge is being guided by the Spirit

*I pray that your love
will keep on growing more and more,
together with true knowledge and
perfect judgment, so that you will be able
to choose what is best.* Philippians 1:9–10

The Spiritual Exercises of Saint Ignatius
contains this guideline for life:
"I believe we were created to share our life
and love with God and other people forever.
I believe that God created all other things
to help us carry out this lofty purpose.
I believe, therefore, that we should use
the other things God created, insofar as
they help us carry out the purpose for which
we were created and to abstain from them
insofar as they hinder us from doing this.
Therefore, we shouldn't prefer, out of hand,
certain things to others, for example,
health to sickness, wealth to poverty,
honor to dishonor, or a long life
to a short one. Our sole norm
for preferring a thing should be
how well it helps us attain the end
for which we were created."

Why do/don't I agree with this statement?

*The strength of a person consists
in finding out the way God is going,
and going that way.* Henry Ward Beecher

Journal

Knowledge is finding God in all things

*"Do not be afraid or discouraged,
for I, the LORD your God,
am with you wherever you go."*
Joshua 1:9

A character in David Hare's play
Racing Demons is an old Anglican priest.
In one scene he is all alone at night
in his darkened church.
He has always loved life—and, occasionally,
a bit too much to drink.
Tonight is one of those occasions.
Holding a single candle,
he moves along slowly, talking to God
about people and why they are so unhappy.
He says to God:
"Why can't people enjoy what they have? . . .
I mean . . . the whole thing's so clear.
You're there. In people's happiness.
Tonight in the taste of drink.
Or the love of my friends.
The whole thing's so simple. . . .
Why do people find it so hard?"

What is the old priest's point?
How would I respond to his question?

*Walking with God
isn't a matter of the intellect;
it's a matter of the heart.*
Joni Eareckson Tada

Journal

Knowledge is loving all things

Whoever does not love does not know God, for God is love. 1 John 4:8

Helen Keller was blind, deaf, and dumb
from childhood. Annie Sullivan became
her teacher and entered her dark world.
One rainy day, Helen asked Annie what love
was like. Years later, Helen recorded
Annie's response this way:
"'Love is something like the clouds. . . .
You cannot touch the clouds . . .
but you feel the rain [pouring from them]
and know how glad the flowers and
the thirsty earth are to have it. . . .
You cannot touch love either, but you feel
the sweetness that it pours into everything."
Helen concluded by describing the effect
this explanation had upon her.
"The beautiful truth [about love]
burst upon my mind—
I felt that there were invisible lines
stretched between my spirit
and the spirits of others." *The Story of My Life*

How do I explain this: The sage says,
"We can't love what we don't know."
The saint says, "It is also true that we
can't know what we don't love." Anonymous

Love is not blind; it is supersighted.
Author unknown

Journal

Journal

Knowledge is focusing on what counts

Those things that I might count as profit
I now reckon as loss. . . .
All I want is to know Christ and to . . .
share in his sufferings and . . . in his death,
in the hope that I myself will be raised
from death to life. Philippians 3:7, 10–11

During his "glory days" in Washington, D.C.,
Daniel Webster used to worship regularly
in a small church outside Washington.
This bothered some of his colleagues.
They thought he should worship
in a prominent church more fitting
to his status as a statesman.
One day, when the subject surfaced
in a conversation, Webster explained
his reason this way:
"When I worship in the prominent churches,
I always get the feeling—right or wrong—
that they are preaching
to Webster, the statesman.
When I worship in that small, obscure church,
I get the feeling that the minister
is preaching to Webster, the sinner."

What are my reasons for worshiping as I do?

*Religion is not a way
of looking at certain things.
It is a certain way
of looking at everything.* Robert E. Segal

Knowledge is keeping priorities straight

Journal

*If the LORD does not build the house,
the work of the builders is useless.*
Psalms 127:1

Years ago, the film *Mr. Deeds Goes to Town*
was a huge box-office success.
Mr. Deeds was a homespun poet
who wrote greeting card verse and played
a tuba in a small-town band in Vermont.
Then his rich uncle dies and he inherits
$20 million. He goes to New York
and is naively unchanged by his fortune.
Crooked lawyers make a play for him.
The directors of the opera elect him
to their board. Soon he grows disillusioned
by the people he meets in the city.
One night he confides to a young woman:
"People here are funny. They work so hard
at living they forget how to live.
Last night, after I left you, I was walking
along and—looking at the tall buildings,
and I got to thinking about what Thoreau said,
'They created a lot of grand palaces here, but they
forgot to create the nobleman to put into them.'"

What point is Mr. Deeds making, and what
might it be saying to me about my life?

*We know next to nothing
about virtually everything.* George F. Will

Gift of Fortitude

Columnist Abigail Van Buren received
a letter from a "nameless" woman.
It thanked her for printing (years ago)
an anonymous poem called "The Dilemma."

The woman explained that
she "had been a prisoner, doing hard time
in the high-walled prison of alcoholism."
The poem gave her the initial courage
to admit her problem and to keep going
to Alcoholics Anonymous.

She ended, saying, "I can't begin to tell you
how many of us this poem has helped,"
and urged her to reprint it. The poem read:

To laugh is to risk appearing a fool.
To weep is to risk appearing sentimental.
To reach out to another is to risk involvement.
To expose feelings is to risk rejection.
To place your dreams before the crowd
is to risk ridicule.
To love is to risk not being loved in return.
To go forward in the face of overwhelming
odds is to risk failure.

But risks must be taken because
the greatest hazard in life is to risk nothing.
The person who risks nothing,
does nothing, has nothing, is nothing.
He may avoid suffering and sorrow,
but he cannot learn, feel, change,

grow or love.
Chained to his certitudes, he is a slave.
He has forfeited his freedom.

Only a person who dares to risk is free.

The poem introduces us
to the Holy Spirit's gift of fortitude.

The gift of fortitude empowers us
to take risks.
It frees us to dream, to love, to reach out—
to "plunge into the deep without fear,
with the gladness of April in our heart."
Rabindranath Tagore

It is the courage to move forward
on our spiritual journey to God
with a quiet perseverance and faith
that only the Holy Spirit can give.

And so
it is to the Holy Spirit's gift of fortitude
that we now turn.

Fortitude is
doing what is right

*[Jesus told a story of a widow who kept
badgering a corrupt judge for her rights.]
"For a long time the judge refused to act,
but at last he said to himself,
'Even though I don't fear God
or respect people,
yet because of all the trouble this widow
is giving me, I will see to it
that she gets her rights.'"* Luke 18:4–5

"There's an ageless message in the rubble
of the crumpled walls of Jericho. . . .
If they make enough noise—loud enough and
long enough—walls of oppression . . .
come tumbling down. . . .
The civil rights movement of the sixties
cracked the walls of fear [and] . . .
spawned the human rights movement.
Women, Puerto Ricans, Chicanos . . .
began to organize and
resist their oppression as never before."
Dick Gregory's Bible Tales with Commentary,
James R. McGraw, ed.

How ready am I to combat injustice,
as did the widow in Jesus' story?

*There may be times
when we are powerless to prevent injustice,
but there must never be a time
when we fail to protest it.* Elie Wiesel

57

Journal

Fortitude is risking failure

*The time is here for me to leave this life.
I have done my best . . .
and I have kept the faith.* 2 Timothy 4:6–7

British explorers Scott, Wilson, and Bowers
were returning from an ill-fated expedition
to Antarctica. A blizzard was raging.
Blinded by the snow, exhausted, and cold,
they pitched a tent in the snowy wasteland.
They were out of food. The end was near.
And they knew it.
Scott faced death with the same courage
he had in facing the failure of his mission.
Barely able to hold a pencil,
he wrote this last message to the world:
"We bow to the will of Providence,
determined still to do our best to the last.
Had we lived, I should have had a tale to tell
of the hardihood, endurance and courage
of my companions, which would have stirred
the heart of every Englishman. These notes
and our dead bodies must tell the tale."
Eight months later, on February 10, 1913,
a search team found the bodies and the note.

How courageously do I face failure?
The prospects of my own death?

*I have the strength to face all conditions
by the power that Christ gives me.*
Philippians 4:13

Fortitude is striving against odds

Journal

Stand firm and steady. . . .
Nothing you do in the Lord's service
is ever useless. 1 Corinthians 15:58

Robert E. Sherwood was a speech writer
for President Franklin Roosevelt.
He also won the Pulitzer prize in drama
three times. On one occasion—
mustering all the drama at his command—
he said we must dedicate ourselves
to two objectives:
the achievement of world peace and
the affirmation of the right of every person
to live as the image of God. He added,
"To those who say that these unlimited
objectives are unthinkable, impossible,
let us reply that it is the alternative
to them which is unthinkable, impossible."
He concluded by calling upon America
to dedicate itself to the achievement
of these unlimited objectives as boldly
and as confidently as our forefathers,
"who proved that . . . nothing undertaken
by free men and free women is impossible."

What positive steps might I take to help
implement Sherwood's two objectives?

When you dream alone, it remains a dream,
but when you dream with others,
it can become a reality. Kahlil Gibran

Fortitude is never quitting

Tell everyone who is discouraged,
"Be strong and don't be afraid!
God is coming to your rescue." Isaiah 35:4

Glenn Van Ekeren gives seminars
on maximizing human potential.
He is fond of telling the story about
a basketball coach who had the rare art
of inspiring teams with the courage to
fight back when things looked impossible.
During the halftime of one difficult game,
he stood before the team and yelled,
"Did Michael Jordan ever quit?"
The team yelled back, "No!"
The coach yelled, "Did Nolan Ryan ever quit?"
The team yelled, "No!"
"What about the Wright brothers.
Did they quit?" "No!" yelled the team.
Then the coach shouted. "And what about
Elmer McAllister. Did he ever quit?"
There was an awkward pause.
Then the team captain said, "Coach,
we never heard of him!" "Of course you didn't!"
shouted the coach. "He quit!"

What motivates me not to quit
when I am tempted to do so?

What we need is more people
who will specialize in the impossible.
Theodore Roethke

Fortitude is
witnessing to the faith

Journal

*Jesus said, "I assure you
that those who declare publicly
that they belong to me,
the Son of Man will do the same for them
before the angels of God.
But those who reject me publicly,
the Son of Man will also reject them
before the angels of God."* Luke 12:8–9

Jim Reily,
a teenager from Croton, New York,
received national publicity
when he resigned his paper route
to protest a sizable abortion ad
in the Sunday edition of the paper.
Bill Molloy
of Cincinnati received similar publicity
when he arranged for an operation
in a hospital that refused abortions—
even though his doctor
was not on the staff of that hospital.
"It's a statement of my beliefs," he said.
Reported in *Christopher News Notes*

Can I recall "a statement of my beliefs"
that I made?
What's the most effective way
to make such a statement?

Problems loom large when men don't.
Robert J. Bidinotto

Journal

Fortitude is not looking back

*Jesus said, "Anyone who starts to plow
and then keeps looking back
is of no use for the Kingdom of God."* Luke 9:62

Years ago there was a popular movie
called *42nd Street,* In it, Warner Baxter
greeted his Broadway chorus line
with this challenging overture:
"All right, everybody.
Be quiet and listen to me.
Tomorrow morning,
we're going to start a show.
We're going to work and
sweat, and work some more. . . .
You're going to dance
until your feet fall off and
you're not able to stand it any longer.
But five weeks from now,
we're going to have a show."

How does this challenging overture
to the chorus line relate to Jesus' words
about not looking back?

*There are three kinds of souls.
One says, "I am a bow in your hands, Lord.
Draw me lest I rot.
The second says,
"Do not overdraw me, Lord. I shall break."
The third says, "Overdraw me and who cares
if I break."* Nikos Kazantzakos, *Report to Greco*

Fortitude is knowing God is at my side

Journal

"Do not be afraid—I am with you!
I am your God—let nothing terrify you!
I will make you strong and help you;
I will protect you and save you."
Isaiah 41:10

Dr. Sheila Cassidy left England
and practiced medicine amongst
the poorest of the poor in Chile.
Then one day she was arrested
by the Chilean secret police
for treating a revolutionary leader.
She was taken into custody, tied down,
and tortured for four days by having
electrodes attached to her body.
When she was eventually released,
she explained her courage this way:
"I think it was the fact
that prayer had become an integral part
of my life before I became a prisoner
that made it possible for me
to face the unknown with a calm
that surprised even me."

What do I fear most as I look to my future?
What does Dr. Cassidy's experience say
to me about that fear and others like it?

Let nothing frighten you. . . .
Who has God, lacks nothing.
God alone is enough. Saint Teresa of Avila

Gift of Counsel

Emily Kingsley is the mother of a child
with a disability. To help people understand
what this is like, she penned a touching
parable entitled. "Welcome to Holland."
It goes something like this:

Planning a baby's birth
is like planning a dream vacation to Italy.
When the joyful day comes, you hug friends,
board the aircraft, and take off.

A few hours later, the plane lands, and
the stewardess says, "Welcome to Holland!"
"Holland!" you say. "I'm going to Italy!
All my life I've dreamed of going to Italy."
"Sorry!" says the flight attendant.
"There's been a change in plans."

You get off the plane—in utter shock.
You can't believe the reversal of events.
Stunned, you leave the airport on a bus.
You look around—dazed.
At least Holland isn't a dreadful place
filled with horrors. It's just different.

So you buy a guide book and set out.
You begin to notice that Holland has
windmills, tulips, and even Rembrandts.
Still, everyone you meet who's seen Italy
raves about what an exciting place it is.
And for the rest of your life, you say,
"That's where I was supposed to vacation.

And the pain of that lost dream lingers
and lingers—and never goes away.

But if you spend the rest of your life
grieving the loss of your broken dream,
you'll never enjoy
the many lovely things Holland has to offer.

Ms. Helen Kingsley's handling of an
unexpectedcrisis situation introduces us
to the Holy Spirit's gift of counsel.

This gift empowers us to discern
the way to handle a "crisis" situation.
And if we are charged with guiding others,
it helps us discern how to "counsel" them
in a similar crisis situation.

Jesus referred to the Holy Spirit's
"gift of counsel" when he told his disciples:

"When they bring you to trial, do not worry
about what you are going to say. . . .
For the words you will speak
will not be yours; they will come
from the Spirit." Matthew 10:19–20

And so it is to the Spirit's gift of counsel
that we now turn.

Counsel
gives us new hope

*[A storm threatened to submerge the boat
in which Jesus and the disciples were sailing.
The disciples shouted to Jesus to save them.
Jesus calmed the storm and asked,]*
"Where is your faith?" Luke 8:25

Gretta Palmer was interviewing novelist
Mary Roberts Rinehart.
She began, "Can you talk about your cancer?"
Mary replied, "I am *glad* to talk about it."
She said that the cancer was in remission
and that she was working better than ever.
That interview gave new hope to people
facing a similar health crisis.
Mary's "counsel" to them was simple.
A "crisis" is a "dangerous opportunity."
It can make you bitter or better,
depending on how you decide to face it.
"The important thing," she said,
"is to face it with courage and faith,
and with the will to survive."

How have I experienced the Spirit's power
guiding me in some crisis situation?

*For every hill I've had to clilmb . . .
For all the blood and sweat and grime . . .
My heart sings but a grateful song—
These were things that made me strong.*
Anonymous

Journal

Counsel is listening to loved ones

Arrogance causes nothing but trouble.
It is wiser to ask for advice. Proverbs 13:10

It's hard to imagine a Christmas program
without "Rudolph the Red-Nosed Reindeer"
being on the music menu.
The story behind the hit goes back 50 years.
After his previous year's blockbuster hit,
"Here Comes Santa Claus," Gene Autry was
looking for a follow-up for the current year.
One day the mail brought a recording
of "Rudolph the Red-Nosed Reindeer."
It was the work of a young songwriter
named Johnny Marks. Autry listened to it,
but he was not keen on it.
His wife, however, "counseled" otherwise.
She felt kids would go for it. They did!
Today, more than 400 artists have recorded it,
and over 100 million copies of the song
have been sold.

I'm not always the best judge of something.
It helps to seek the counsel of others.
How readily do I seek the counsel of others?
How do I decide whose counsel to follow?

You should be careful
to observe the way
toward which your heart draws you;
then choose this way with all your strength.
Martin Buber

Counsel is interpreting events

Jesus said, "You can look at the earth and the sky and predict the weather; why, then, don't you know the meaning of this present time?" Luke 12:56

The world watched on TV
as astronauts Neil Armstrong and Ed Aldrin
landed on the moon on July 20, 1969.
Six hours later, both men were walking
on its powderlike surface.
Later, Aldrin said of the scientific feat
of landing someone on the moon:
"It was more than a team
of people and government and industry
working together. . . . It is my hope
that people will keep this whole event
in their minds and see beyond the minor
details and technical achievements
to the deeper meaning behind it all:
a challenge, a quest, the human need
to recognize that we are all one mankind
under God." *Life* magazine (July 20, 1969)

What deeper meaning might the scientific
feat of landing someone on the moon
hold for our nation? For our world?

In the swift rush of great events, we find ourselves groping to know the full sense and meaning of these times in which we live. Dwight D. Eisenhower

67

Journal

Counsel is forgetting certain things

We use the tongue to give thanks . . .
and also to curse other people. . . .
Words of thanksgiving and cursing
pour out from the same mouth.
My friends, this should not happen!
James 3:9–10

"If you see a tall fellow ahead of a crowd, /
A leader of men, marching fearless and
proud, / And you know of a tale whose mere
telling aloud / Would cause his proud head
in anguish be bowed, /
It's a pretty good plan to forget it. //
If you know of a skeleton hidden away /
In a closet, and guarded, and kept
from day / In the dark, and whose showing,
whose sudden display / Would cause grief
and sorrow and pain and dismay/
It's a pretty good plan to forget it. //
If you know of a tale that will darken the
joy/ Of a man or a woman, a girl or a boy, /
That will wipe out a smile or the least bit
Annoy / A fellow, or cause any gladness
to cloy, / It's a pretty good plan to forget it."
Judd Mortimer Lewis, "Forget It"

To what extent do I use my power of speech
to harm or hurt people in some way?

If you judge people, you have no time
to love them. Mother Teresa

Counsel is
discerning situations

[One] night the LORD appeared
to Solomon in a dream and asked him,
"What would you like me to give you?"
Solomon answered, ". . . O LORD God,
you have let me succeed my father as king,
even though I am very young and don't know
how to rule. . . . Give me the wisdom I need
to rule your people." 1 Kings 3:5–7, 9

Not long after Solomon had this dream,
he was faced with a difficult case.
Two women laid claim
to being the mother of the same infant son.
To learn who the true mother was,
Solomon said to an attendant,
" 'Cut the living child in two
and give each woman half of it.' "
The real mother,
her heart full of love for her son,
said to the king,.'. . . Don't kill the child!
Give it to her.' " 1 Kings 3:25–26

In making decisions,
how regularly do I pray to the Holy Spirit
for "counsel" or "guidance"?
Why don't I seek the Spirit's help
more regularly and more confidently?

Wisdom is knowing what to do. . . .
Skill is knowing how to do it.
Virtue is doing it. Thomas Jefferson

Counsel is knowing when not to try harder

Any who love knowledge
want to be told when they are wrong.
It is stupid to hate being corrected.
Proverbs 12:1

Price Prichett was watching a fly
burn out its last bit of life energy
trying to fly through the glass
of a windowpane.
Its whirring wings communicated
the fly's strategy: simply try harder.
But the strategy was the wrong one.
The fly was doomed to die of exhaustion.
Meanwhile, across the room,
a door stood open to the out-of-doors.
Why didn't the fly head for the door?
Why didn't it try a different strategy
to achieve its goal?
Sometimes "trying harder" is not
the right strategy to achieve a goal.
The gift of counsel helps us discern
when to "try harder"
and when to use a different strategy.

How might this gift apply to me right now?

God, give me the serenity
to accept what I can't change,
the courage to change what I can,
and the wisdom to know the difference.
Reinhold Niebuhr (slightly adapted)

Journal

Counsel is
staying in control

*Even though our physical being is gradually
decaying, yet our spiritual being
is renewed day after day.* 2 Corinthians 4:16

Psychologist Julius Segal worked with
the 52 Americans held captive by Iran
for 444 days in the early 1980s.
He listed four reasons why some of them
not only survived the ordeal
but grew stronger as a result of it.
First, they resisted the temptation
to withdraw into themselves.
Second, they helped other captives.
Shifting attention from their own woes
and reaching out to help others
had a remarkable healing effect on them.
Third, they kept control of their lives.
One captive invited his guards to sit down
each time they entered his room. "This was
my space," he said. "They were my guests."
This tiny gesture helped him stay in control
and resist becoming a passive victim.
Lastly, they learn to tap inner powers
through prayer and meditation.

Which of these four guidelines have I found
most helpful in crisis situations?

*Start by doing what's necessary;
then do what's possible; and suddenly
you are doing the impossible.* Saint Francis of Assisi

Gift of Understanding

The French genius Blaise Pascal
designed and built computing machines
that were pioneers of today's computer.

He pushed his intellectual powers
to the limit. It was there,
at the limit of human reason,
that he grew restless and longed for
a deeper understanding of the reality
and truth of his Christian faith.

One night, it came unexpectedly,
as he describes in his journal.
Here are excerpts from it:

Monday, November 23, 1654,
from about half past ten in the evening
until half past midnight:
Fire . . . certainty, joy, peace! . . .
Jesus Christ. . . .
Sweet and total renunciation.
Total submission to Jesus Christ. . . .
Tears of joy!
I had parted from him.
Let me never again be separated from him.

These excerpts from Pascal introduce us
to the Spirit's gift of understanding:
a profound, heartfelt grasp
of the deeper meaning and beauty
of God's revelation to us.

The gift of understanding is linked
to the virtue of faith,
but differs from it in an important way.

Faith empowers us to say yes to
the truthfulness of God's cosmic word
(creation), inspired word (Scripture),
and Incarnate Word (Jesus).
The gift of understanding empowers us
to penetrate its deeper meaning and beauty.

An example of this gift of empowerment
is the psalmist who cries out joyfully:

O LORD . . .
How I love your law! . . .
How sweet is the taste
of your instructions—
sweeter even than honey! Psalms 119:89, 97, 103

This appreciation of God's revelation to us
is often so intense that it produces
what Saint Paul calls a "fruit of the Spirit."

An example is the "joy" that Pascal
experienced on his memorable night.

And so this week's meditations focus on
the gift of understanding,
which moved Pascal
to a total commitment to Jesus Christ.

Understanding is seeing with the heart

Jesus said, "Whatever you did for one of the least important of these followers of mine, you did it for me!" Matthew 25:40

An editorial began: "A priest we know recently described his experience of being confronted by a beggar while eating at a fast-food restaurant. The beggar said he was hungry, and the priest, intimidated and nervous, could only say, 'I'm sorry,' and look the other way. Later, as the priest recounted the story, he was praying Psalm 80, 'Lord, let me see your face,' when the image of the beggar came to mind. How many times have we seen the Lord and not recognized him? . . . Christ simply appears before us: hungry, cold and ill. Once He was a condemned prisoner led to the slaughter for the sins of others. Now he approaches us in McDonald's smelling badly. . . . Do we see his face?"
Editorial in *Our Sunday Visitor* (Dec. 15, 1996)

What keeps me from seeing Jesus' face more clearly in people around me?

Beware of the man whose God is in the skies. G. B. Shaw

Journal

Understanding is serenity entering the soul

Jesus said, "The Spirit . . .
will lead you into all the truth." John 16:13

In 1858 a girl named Bernadette reported apparitions of Mary at a hillside in Lourdes, France. Sick people visited the site and were cured. Over 1,300 cures are well documented. In the 1930s Alexis Carrel, a skeptical New York surgeon and Nobel prize winner, went to Lourdes to investigate the claims. While there, he witnessed a girl being cured. He stood in silence, totally stunned. That night he went for a long walk. Ending up in a church, he prayed: "I still doubt. . . . Beneath . . .intellectual pride a smothered dream persists . . . the dream of believing."
He returned to his hotel and recorded his observations. In *The Voyage to Lourdes,* he describes what then happened: "A new coolness penetrated the open window. I felt the serenity of nature enter my soul with gentle calm. All intellectual doubts had vanished."

How do I understand such miracles?

For those who believe in God no explanation is necessary. For those who do not believe, no explanation is possible. Author unknown

Understanding is
praying from the heart

Jesus said,
"If one of you wants to be great,
you must be the servant of the rest. . . .
The Son of Man . . . did not come
to be served, but to serve and to give
his life to redeem many people." Matthew 20:26, 28

On Thursday evening, April 12, 1945,
radio stations interrupted all broadcasts
to announce President Roosevelt's death.
It was critical, because World War II
was at a crucial point.
Harry Truman was sworn in.
Later, Truman addressed Congress.
His final words were dramatic.
He lifted his face upward,
raised his arms to heaven and said,
"I humbly pray Almighty God,
in the words of King Solomon:
'Give me . . . an understanding heart
to judge Thy people, that I may discern
between good and bad.' . . .
I ask only to be a good and faithful servant
of my Lord and my people."

How can I become a more faithful servant
of "my Lord and my people"?

The greatest reward for serving others
is the satisfaction found in your own heart.
E. C. McKenzie

75

Journal

_____

_____

_____

_____

_____

_____

_____

_____

_____

_____

_____

Understanding is feeling with the heart

"I will light the lamp of understanding in your heart, and it will not go out."
2 Esdras 14:25

Madame Chiang Kai-shek was the wife
of the founder of modern Taiwan.
One day she was reading the gospel passage
where a soldier pierces the side of Jesus.
She had read it many times before,
without being particularly moved by it.
But this time was different. She writes:
"I realized that His suffering and pain
were for me. I cried and cried. . . . I seldom
weep, for as children we were trained not
to show emotion. But this was a torrent,
like a flood. I could not control it.
At the same time, my heart felt light and
relieved, feeling that my sins were washed
away with those tears. . . . Thenceforth
I was not only intellectually convinced
but personally attached to my Lord."
"The Power of Prayer" in *Reader's Digest* (Aug. 1955)

How intellectually and personally attached am I
to Jesus as my Lord, my God, and my Savior?

*God sometimes washes the eyes
of his children with tears,
in order that they may read aright
his providence and his commandments.*
Theodore Ledyard Cuyler

Understanding is seeing more deeply

Jesus said, "You can predict the weather by looking at the sky, but you cannot interpret the signs concerning these times!"
Matthew 16:3

An Arabian parable describes a horseman
galloping through the night
toward the City of the Sun,
which lies on the other side of the valley.
Suddenly he hears a voice shout,
"Halt! Dismount! Pick up some pebbles!
Put them in your pocket. Tomorrow
at sunrise you'll be both sad and glad."
The horseman obeyed.
This happened several more times.
Finally, the horseman came to the valley
and began to descend. The path was steep
and the stones began pinching his leg,
so he began throwing them away one by one.
About sunrise he came to the other side
of the valley. As he did, he reached into his
pocket to throw away the last stone,
which was pinching his leg. It felt strange.
He looked and saw that it had turned into
a diamond. He was both sad and glad.

Why was the horseman both sad and glad?
What message might the story hold for me?

Problems are only opportunities with thorns on them. Hugh Miller

Journal

Understanding is knowing your "cannots"

Kind words bring life, but cruel words crush your spirit. Proverbs 15:4

"You cannot bring about prosperity
by discouraging thrift.
You cannot help small men
by tearing down big men. . . .
You cannot lift the wage earner
by pulling down the wage payer.
You cannot help the poor man
by destroying the rich.
You cannot keep out of trouble
by spending more than your income.
You cannot further the brotherhood of man
by inciting class hatred.
You cannot establish security
on borrowed money.
You cannot build character and courage
by taking away
men's initiative and independence.
You cannot help men permanently
by doing for them what they could and
should do for themselves."
William J. H. Boetcker, "Ten Cannots"

Which of the above "cannots" is a problem
in today's world? Which am I most guilty of?

*Two things are bad for the heart—
running up stairs and running down people.*
Bernard Baruch

Understanding is
touching a flower

O LORD, our Lord,
your greatness is seen in all the world!
Psalms 8:1

The Vietnamese monk and apostle of peace
Thich Nhat Hanh writes:
"Whenever I touch a flower,
I touch the sun and yet, I do not get burned!
When I touch the flower,
I touch a cloud flying to the sky. . . .
If you really touch one flower deeply,
you touch the whole cosmos."
Cultivating the Mind of Love

It is against this background
that Father Ernesto Cardinal says:
"Only dimly
do we understand the nature of things.
What are things?
They are God's love become things.
God also communicates with us
by way of all things.
They are messages of love. . . .
Everything I enjoy was given lovingly
by God for me to enjoy."

What keeps me from seeing all things
as "God's love become things"?

Help me look at raindrops and see oceans.
Help me look at time and see eternity.
Elizabeth Coatsworth

Gift of Wisdom

A woman was inside a house,
seated by a window, reading a book.
Outside the weather was cold and gray.
All of a sudden, a ray of sunlight
pierced the clouds, penetrated the window,
and fell across her hands and arm.

The brightness and warmth
of that solitary sunbeam filled her with joy.
A few seconds before she felt depressed.
Now she was overflowing with joy.

Perhaps it was an experience like this
that led a 20th-century spiritual writer
to compare the gift of wisdom
to a sunbeam, saying:

*It is a ray of light
illuminating the eye of soul,
filling it with delight; and
a ray of heat warming the human heart,
flooding it with joy.* Adolph Tanquerey

The gift of wisdom enables us to discern
and relish God's presence in all things.
It does more.
It gives us a profound appreciation of the way
everything on earth and in heaven
fits together in a magnificent symphony
of beauty and harmony.

This week's meditations focus on
this gift of wisdom
and the delight that it brings the soul.

In preparation for the meditations,
it might be good to review the traditional
"Seven Gifts of the Holy Spirit."

Fear of the LORD draws us from sin to God.

Piety awakens in us the awesome mystery
of God and God's love for us.

Knowledge helps us see how everything
comes from God and leads us back to God.

Fortitude strengthens us to pursue our
journey to God joyfully and courageously.

Counsel helps us discern the right course
of action, especially in difficult situations.

Understanding empowers us to penetrate
more deeply into the meaning and beauty
of God's revelation.

Wisdom enables us to discern and relish
God's presence in all things—and to see how
they fit together in a divine symphony of love.

Let us now turn to this week's meditations
on the Holy Spirit's gift of wisdom.

Wisdom is seeing his face in every flower

Journal

*Even birds and animals
have much they could teach you. . . .
All of them know that the LORD'S hand
made them.* Job 12:7, 9

The gift of wisdom opens our eyes
to see the divine reflection mirrored
in every flower on earth, every star in the sky,
every bird in flight, every wave on the sea.
The poet sings:
"I see His blood upon the rose
And in the stars the glory of His eyes,
His Body gleams amid eternal snows,
His tears fall from the skies. //
I see His face in every flower;
The thunder and the singing of the birds
Are but His voice—and carven by His power
Rocks are His written words. //
All pathways by His feet are worn,
His strong heart stirs the ever-beating sea,
His crown of thorns is twined
with every thorn, / His cross is every tree."
Joseph Mary Plunkett, "I See His Blood upon the Rose"

What keeps me from seeing God mirrored
more clearly in nature? In people?
What might I do to improve my vision?

*Earth is but the frozen echo
of the silent voice of God.*
Samuel Hagesman

Wisdom is being held in God's hand

Your hands formed and shaped me. . . .
You have given me life and constant love.
Job 10:8, 12

"We're in His hand, that mighty hand,
that flung a universe in space . . .
That guides the sun and moon and stars,
and holds the planets in their place. . . . //
We're in His hand, that skillful hand,
that made the blinded eyes to see . . .
That touched the leper, cleansed and healed,
and set the palsied sufferer free. . . . //
We're in that hand, that loving hand,
that lifted children to His breast . . .
That fed the hungry multitudes
and beckoned weary hearts to rest. . . . //
We're in His hands, those pierced hands,
once nailed to Calvary's cruel tree . . .
When there in agony and blood
He paid the price to set us free." Author unknown

What keeps me from greater trust in God?

The same everlasting Father
who cares for you today will take care
of you tomorrow and every day.
Either he will shield you from suffering,
or he will give you unfailing strength
to bear it. Be at peace then and put aside
all anxious thoughts and imaginations.
Saint Francis de Sales

Journal

Wisdom is seeing God in all things

Journal

You tell us to return to what we were;
you change us back to dust. . . .
Our life . . . fades away like a whisper. . . .
Teach us how short our life is,
so that we may become wise. Psalms 90:3, 9, 12

"My heart was heavy, for its trust had been
Abused, its kindness answered
with foul wrong;
So turning gloomily from my fellow men,
One summer Sabbath day I strolled among
The green mounds of the village burial-place;
Where, pondering how all human love and hate
Find one sad level; and how, soon or late,
Wronged and wrongdoer,
each with meekened face,
And cold hands folded over a still heart,
Pass the green threshold of our common grave,
Whither all footsteps tend, whence none depart,
Awed for myself, and pitying my race,
Our common sorrow, like a mighty wave,
Swept all my pride away, and, trembling,
I forgave!" John Greenleaf Whittier

What does death say to me
about the relationship between
the temporal realities of this world and
the eternal realities of the next world?

Once you accept your own death
all of a sudden you're free to live. Saul Alinsky

Journal

Wisdom is trusting in God totally

God's foolishness is wiser than human wisdom, and . . . God's weakness is stronger than human strength. 1 Corinthians 1:25

The film *War of the Worlds* is based on H. G. Wells's novel. It describes the invasion of earth by one-eyed, froglike Martians. When all seems lost for humanity and terror sweeps the earth, the invasion suddenly and mysteriously collapses. The story ends with the narrator explaining the "miracle." "The Martians had no resistance to bacteria in our atmosphere to which we have long since become immune. Once they had breathed our air, germs which no longer affect us began to kill them. Their machines began to stop and fall. After all man could do had failed, the Martians were destroyed and humanity saved by the littlest things God in his wisdom put on this earth."

How do I reconcile the evil in our world with the wisdom of God?

I proclaim . . . God's secret wisdom . . . It was to us that God made known his secret by means of his Spirit. . . . God has made Christ to be our wisdom.
1 Corinthians 2:7, 10; 1:30

Wisdom is believing in God's providence

*Give yourself to the LORD;
trust in him, and he will help you.* Psalms 37:5

The film *Cocoon*
centers around the return of aliens to earth
to retrieve 20 crew members who,
in an emergency, had to be left behind
on a prior mission in suspended animation
in underwater cocoons.
The fun starts when elderly members
of a retirement community find the cocoons
and begin exploring them. They experience
a physical and a spiritual rejuvenation.
The film ends with a minister consoling
the members on the loss of some friends.
He says:
"There can never be an accounting . . .
for the tragedy at sea which has taken
the lives of these men and women
in what should have been the beautiful and
peaceful sunset of their lives. Do not fear.
Your loved ones are in safekeeping. They
have moved to a higher expression of life."

How do I reconcile the wisdom of God
with tragedy and death?

*Trust the past to God's mercy,
the present to God's love,
and the future to God's providence.*
Saint Augustine

Journal

Wisdom is praying for guidance

Jesus said, "Ask, and you will receive;
seek, and you will find;
knock, and the door will be opened to you.
For those who ask will receive,
and those who seek will find,
and the door will be opened to anyone
who knocks." Luke 11:9–10

President Truman prayed this prayer
regularly throughout his entire life:
"O Almighty and Everlasting God,
Creator of Heaven, Earth, and the Universe.
Help me to be, to think, to act what is right,
because it is right; make me truthful,
honest, and honorable in all things;
make me intellectually honest for the sake
of right and honor, and without thought
of reward to me.
Give me the ability to be charitable,
forgiving, and patient with my fellowmen—
help me to understand their motives
and their shortcomings—
even as Thou understandest mine!
Amen, Amen, Amen."

What is one prayer I pray regularly? Why?

He prayeth best who loveth best
All things both great and small;
For the dear Lord, who loveth us,
He made and loveth all. Samuel Taylor Coleridge

Wisdom is knowing
God is in control

*After the supper, Jesus took the cup
and said, "This cup is God's new covenant,
sealed with my blood."* 1 Corinthians 11:25

The movie *The Silver Chalice* refers to the
cup Jesus drank from at the Last Supper.
It was stolen and disappeared into history.
Interwoven into the movie is a subplot,
centering on Simon the magician (Acts 8:18).
In the film (not the Bible), he climbs a tower
and jumps to his death, seeking to fly
and thereby prove he is the Messiah.
The film ends with Peter saying of the cup:
"It will be restored. But for years and
hundreds of years, it will lie in darkness,
where I know not. When it is brought out
into the light again, there will be
great cities and mighty bridges. . . .
It will be a world of evil and bitter wars. . . .
But it may be in that age,
when a man holds lightning in his hands
and rides the sky as Simon the magician
strove to do, it will be needed more
than it is needed now."

What purpose would the "silver chalice"
serve in our time? Had badly is it needed?

*Our hearts have a God-shaped hole
in them that only God can fill.* Author unknown

Fruit of Love

A king wished to learn
which of his three sons was the wisest
and the best qualified to succeed him.
So he devised a test.

He took his eldest son on a daylong hike.
At noon, after they had eaten lunch,
the king said, "My son, I feel a bit tired.
How can we shorten our trip home?"
The son said, "Father, we came by the
shortest route possible. We can't shorten it."

A week later the king took his second son
on the same trip. After lunch he posed
the same question. The son replied, "Father,
we came by the shortest route possible.
We can't shorten it."

A week later the king took his youngest son
on the same trip. After lunch the king said,
"My son, I feel a bit tired. How can we
shorten our trip home?" The son said,
"Father, let me think about that a minute.
Meanwhile let's start back."

Shortly the son said,
"Father, tell me about the enjoyable times
you had with your friends
as you walked along this same road
when you were my age."
The king began recalling story after story.

He got so involved in recalling the stories
that the trip was over in a flash.

Suddenly the king realized what his son had
done. He said, "My son, your loving concern
for me not only shortened our trip
but gave the strength I needed to make it."

This week's meditations focus on love,
the first "fruit" of the Holy Spirit.

Recall that Christian tradition says that
when we live in harmony with the "virtues"
and the "gifts" of the Spirit,
we are blessed with a variety of "fruits."

In other words, we experience
a divine influx of "love, joy, peace,
patience, kindness, generosity,
faithfulness, gentleness, and self-control."
Galatians 5:22–23

These "fruits" of the Spirit
act as a kind of earthly preview
of the harmony and happiness
that will characterize our heavenly life.

And so this week's meditation
focuses on the "fruit" of love—
an experience of the harmony and happiness
that comes from being sensitive
to the needs of others and loving them
as Jesus loved us.

Love is a rainbow of many colors

*It is love, then,
that you should strive for.*
1 Corinthians 14:1

Saint Paul lists nine fruits of the Spirit.
At the top of the list, he puts love.
And he puts it there for a good reason.
In a true sense, the other eight fruits
are simply colors in the rainbow of love.
Joy is love making music in the heart.
Peace is love basking in God's blessings.
Patience is love willing to wait.
Kindness is love smiling and welcoming.
Generosity is love giving itself away.
Faithfulness is love never growing weary.
Gentleness is love melting hearts.
Self-control is love staying in shape.

How well am I expressing love?
For example, how well am I walking
the second mile, mirroring the master,
mending what I touch, staying the course?

*It is love all the way;
love at the top,
love at the bottom,
and love all the way along
down this list of graces.
If we only just brought forth
the fruit of the Spirit,
what a world we would have!* Dwight L. Moody

Journal

_____

_____

_____

_____

_____

_____

_____

_____

_____

_____

_____

Love is having a jar of pickled cauliflower

The LORD says, ". . . Why spend money
on what does not satisfy? . . .
Listen to me and do what I say, and you
will enjoy the best food of all." Isaiah 55:1–2

In her book *A Marriage Made in Heaven,*
the late Erma Bombeck describes how she
fantasized about her 25th-wedding anniversary.
It goes something like this:
"I pictured a large white tent
with hundreds of guests milling around.
The orchestra was playing our song,
as my husband and I swayed gracefully
on the dance floor."
Actually it turned out very differently.
Her kids threw a couple of hamburgers
on the grill, gulped them down, and split—
leaving her and her husband to clean up.
After her husband put away the last things,
he came over and said affectionately,
"Close your eyes. I have a surprise for you."
When she opened them, she sat holding a jar
of cauliflower, packed in pickle juice.
Her husband said softly,
"I hid it from the kids, because I know
you like cauliflower packed in pickle juice."
Erma concludes, "Maybe love is that simple."

Few happinesses equal the joy
of finding a heart that understands.
Victor Robinsoll (slightly adapted)

Love is giving from the heart

The mountains and hills may crumble,
but my love for you will never end. . . .
So says the LORD who loves you. Isaiah 54:10

Dr. Jonas Salk won fame
for developing a polio vaccine in 1953.
His brother, Dr. Lee Salk, wrote
a popular book, called *My Father, My Son.*
He began the book
by describing a touching scene
between his father and himself.
He writes:
"One blustery winter afternoon in 1944,
my father waited with me in Penn Station
for the train that would take me away
to the army center where I would begin
my World War II military service.
He looked at me with tears
clouding his eyes, hugged me tightly,
kissed me on the cheek and
told me good-bye in a choked voice.
Then, wanting to give me something . . .
he took off his watch and gave it to me."

When did I feel the love of a parent or
a child as deeply as Lee Salk and his father
felt for each other? How did I show it?

Two people who love each other
are in a place more holy
than the interior of a church. William Lyon Phelps

Journal

Love is claiming my power and my glory

If I have no love, I am nothing. 1 Corinthians 13:2

Talk-show hostess Oprah Winfrey
has a wonderful way with her guests.
Her honesty relaxes them, and it's not rare
for her to cry with them right on the show.
Her great compassion comes from the fact
that she suffered greatly in her early life.
Small wonder that the graduation class
of all-female Spelman College
was moved so deeply when she told them:
"My prayer is that you will stop wasting time
being mundane and mediocre.
We are daughters of God—
here to teach the world how to love. . . .
It doesn't matter what you've been through,
where you come from,
who your parents are. . . . What matters
is how you choose to love, how you choose
to express that love through . . .
what you have to give to the world.
Be a queen. Own your power and your glory!"

What is my power and my glory?
What tends to keep me from claiming it—
and expressing it lovingly?

Love is a fabric which never fades,
no matter how often it is washed
in the water of adversity and grief.
E. C. McKenzie

Love is wishing peanuts were emeralds

Journal

These three remain: faith, hope, and love; and the greatest of these is love.
1 Corinthians 13:13

Helen Hayes was not yet a famous actress when she met her future husband, Charlie MacArthur. She writes: "I was at a party feeling very shy because there were a lot of celebrities around, and I was sitting in a corner alone and a very beautiful young man came up to me and offered me some salted peanuts and said [as he handed me the peanuts], 'I wish they were emeralds'; and that was the end of my heart. I never got it back."
Toward the end of her famous life, Helen was sitting alone again. This time an older Charlie came up to her, gave her a handful of emeralds, and said, "I wish these were peanuts."

When did I experience love, as Helen did? When did I last express love, as Charlie did?

He came into my life as the warm wind of spring awakened the flowers, as the April showers awaken the earth. My love for him was unchanging . . . strong as death.
Anna Chennault

Journal

_____
_____
_____
_____
_____
_____
_____
_____
_____
_____

Love is relishing "the giving"

*[Some soldiers heard David say he'd love
a drink of water from a certain well.
They sneaked through the enemy's lines,]
drew some water from the well, and
brought it back to David. But he . . . poured it
out as an offering to the LORD and said,
"I could never drink this! It would be like
drinking the blood of these men
who risked their lives!"* 1 Chronicles 11:18–19

An old story concerns a king's loyal subject.
He came upon a spring of delicious water.
After filling his leather canteen with it,
he began the daylong journey home
to present it to the king.
The king drank it with great relish
and thanked him profusely.
After the subject left, the king's advisor
asked for permission to taste the water.
When he did, he nearly spit it out,
because it was tepid and terribly stale.
He turned to the king and asked,
"Why did you pretend to relish the water?"
The king replied, "It wasn't the water that
I was relishing; it was the subject's love."

How do I respond to the overtures of love
that people (especially family) show me?

*God doesn't want our deeds; God wants
the love that prompts them.* Teresa of Avila

Love is declaring
hearts trump

Jesus said,
"Love your enemies,
do good to those who hate you . . .
and pray for those who mistreat you. . . .
If you love only the people who love you,
why should you receive a blessing?
Even sinners love those who love them!"
Luke 6:27–28, 32

"When we hate our enemies,
we give them power over us—
power over our sleep, our appetite
and our happiness.
They would dance with joy if they knew
how much they were worrying us.
Our hate is not hurting them at all,
but it is turning our own days and nights
into hellish turmoil."
Dale Carnegie, *How to Stop Worrying and Start Living*

Why do I sometimes find it difficult
to love as Jesus said we should love?

In this death and life game of high stakes
God has already, as it were,
declared what are trumps.
They are not
clubs (sheer blind force),
diamonds (the power of wealth), or even
spades (dogged hard work),
but hearts. R. C. Walls, *Asking Them Questions*

Fruit of Joy

Seneca was a famous statesman
who lived in Rome about the same time
that Saint Paul was in prison there.

That era of Roman history
was not too unlike our own today.
It, too, was the dawn of a new millennium.
It, too, was an era of hopeful dreaming.
And one of the dreams was
that the human family would discover
the key to what Christian tradition
calls joy or inner contentment.

Many thinking people in Rome, however,
like Seneca and Saint Paul, feared
that dream was doomed from the outset.
This was because most people of the time
assumed that the key to joy
lay in the pursuit of material wealth and
enjoying the fruit of possessing things.

In his writings, Seneca tried
to redirect people's thinking, saying:

True joy is serene. . . .
The seat of it is within. . . .
It is an invincible greatness of mind
not to be elevated or dejected
by good or ill fortune.

We don't know how familiar
Paul was with the writings of Seneca,
but we do know Paul's thinking
moved in the same direction as Seneca's.

Under divine guidance, Paul taught
that the key to true joy and contentment
lay not in responsiveness
to what our human nature wants,
but in responsiveness
to what the Holy Spirit wants. He writes:

What our human nature wants
is opposed to what the Spirit wants. . . .
Do not deceive yourselves. . . .
You will reap exactly what you plant.

If you plant
in the field of your natural desires,
from it you will gather
the harvest of death;
if you plant in the field of the Spirit,
from the Spirit you will gather
the harvest of eternal life.

So let us not become tired of doing good;
for if we do not give up,
the time will come
when we will reap the harvest. Galatians 5:17, 6:7–9

This week's meditations focus on
the key to inner joy and contentment:
responsiveness to the Holy Spirit,
not to our natural desires.

Joy is being at peace with myself

Journal

Jesus said, "I have told you this so that my joy may be in you and that your joy may be complete." John 15:11

Sydney Piddington wrote an article called "The Special Joys of Super-Slow Reading." In it he says he first tasted these "joys" while a prisoner of war in Singapore. He writes: "I was 19, an artillery sergeant, when the city fell to the Japanese. Waiting with other Australian POWs, I stuffed into my pack a copy of Lin Yutang's *The Importance of Living.* Once in prison, Piddington spent hours meditating on passages in Lin Yutang's book. One passage, especially, spoke to him. It concerned the source of inner joy. Lin Yutang wrote: "The secret of contentment is the discovery by every man of his own powers and limitations. . . . So much restlessness is due to the fact that a man . . . wants too many things."

How does this passage about the secret of contentment or inner joy speak to me right now in my life?

A humble knowledge of myself is a surer way to God than a search after learning. Thomas à Kempis

Journal

Joy is being at peace with God

Do not take your holy spirit away from me.
Give me again the joy that comes
from your salvation. Psalms 51:11–12

John Eagan was making a school retreat.
On the last day, he spent a long time
preparing to make his peace with God.
To his surprise,
the priest didn't speak to him of his sins—
only of God's love for him.
Deeply moved, he walked out into the beauty
of the afternoon. He writes:
"Joy began to well up and run in my heart . . .
growing and surging in me. . . .
I don't think I'd been happier in my life.
I wandered along, wondering at it all.
At length I found myself way out
on the golf course. I remember lying down out of
sheer joy on a bunker
with my eyes to the blue sky
and my arms wide open to the Lord . . . joyful
beyond all bounds.
How long I lay there I don't remember.
All I do remember is
that I felt . . . close to God. *A Traveller toward*
the Dawn: The Spiritual Journal of John Eagan, S.J.

When was one time I felt like John Eagan?

Tears may flow in the night,
but joy comes in the morning. Psalms 30:5

Joy is helping and being helped

Journal

Every time I pray for you all,
I pray with joy because of the way
in which you have helped me. Philippians 1:4–5

Helen Keller was
blind, deaf, and dumb from childhood.
Two people helped her
out of this world of despair and darkness:
Annie Sullivan, who taught her to speak
using her fingers, and
Miss Fuller, who taught her to speak
using her voice.
Helen recalls the joy of learning to speak
using her voice.
She writes in *The Story of My Life:*
"When I had made speech my own,
I could not wait to go home. . . .
My eyes fill with tears now as I think
how my mother pressed me close to her. . . .
It was as if Isaiah's prophecy
had been fulfilled in me,
'The mountains and hills shall break forth
before you into singing, and the trees
of the field shall clap their hands!' "

What was a moment of great joy in my life?

Grief can take care of itself,
but to get the full value of joy
you must have somebody to divide it with.
Mark Twain

Journal

Joy is burning with love

We write this in order that our joy may be complete. 1 John 1:4

British TV celebrity Malcolm Muggeridge wrote a book about Mother Teresa of Calcutta. He called it *Something Beautiful for God.* In it he quotes Mother Teresa as saying: "A joyful heart is the normal result of a heart burning with love. Never let anything so fill you with sorrow as to make you forget the joy of Christ Risen. We long for heaven with him right now— to be happy with him at this very moment. But being happy with him now means: loving as he loves, helping as he helps, giving as he gives, serving as he serves, rescuing as he rescues, being with him twenty-four hours, touching him in his distressing disguise."

Loving, helping, giving, serving, rescuing, being with him, touching his sick—which of these do I find hardest? Easiest? Why?

This is the secret of joy. We shall no longer strive for our own way; but commit ourselves, easily and simply, to God's way. Evelyn Underhill

Joy is redefining the key goal of life

"As fresh water brings joy to the thirsty, so God's people rejoice when he saves them." Isaiah 12:3

"No age in history has been so feverishly occupied with success. . . . For half a century it has been taught by both precept and example that material success—acquisition of fame and money, position and power—is the most important goal in life. . . . We have been proved wrong."
Louis Binstock, The Road to Successful Living

"Many people, in their rise to success, are so busy running to the top, stepping on competitors . . . and saddest of all, stepping on friends and loved ones, that when they get to the top, they look around and discover they are extremely lonely and unhappy. They'll ask me, 'Where did I go wrong?' " Berry Gordy, former president of Motown Industries in the New York Times (Jan. 14, 1979)

Saint Augustine answers the question "Where did I go wrong?" this way: "You were pursuing the wrong goal. The human heart was made for God and it will not rest until it rests in God."

What is Augustine's point?

Joy is the echo of God's life within us.
Joseph Marmion

Journal

Journal

Joy is basking in God's sunlight

Sing to the LORD, all the world!
Worship the LORD with joy.
Psalms 100:1–2

A college girl said, "I'd always thought
that 'pleasure,' 'happiness,' and 'joy'
were different words for the same reality.
Then, one day, I read in *How to Believe:*
"The Holy Spirit . . . helps me
to distinguish pleasure from happiness
and develop real joy.
There are many experiences
which give temporary pleasure
but do not add up to abiding satisfaction.
The thrills pass quickly, and sometimes
leave a trail of regret and remorse.
Some of our sense pleasures
are lightning flashes,
while true joy is like the sunlight."
Ralph W. Sockman, *How to Believe*

What is the difference between pleasure,
happiness, and joy?

Joy is the reverse of happiness.
Happiness is the result
of what happens of an agreeable sort.
Joy has it springs deep down inside.
And that spring
never runs dry, no matter what happens.
Only Jesus gives joy. Samuel Dickey Gordon

Joy is suffering for Jesus

Journal

[After being beaten for preaching Jesus, the apostles left,] rejoicing that they had been found worthy to suffer. Acts 5:41 (NAB)

A second-century story concerns a king who tried to get an influential subject to denounce Jesus. The king said, "If you don't reject your Jesus, I will be forced to banish you." The subject replied, "My dear king, you can't banish me from Jesus. He remains with his followers forever." The king showed irritation and said, "If you don't denounce this Jesus, I'll seize everything you treasure." The subject said, "The only thing I truly treasure is stored in heaven. There's no way you can seize it." The king erupted and shouted, "You leave me no choice but to kill you." The subject said, "My dear king, I am already dead. I died with Jesus in baptism and share his own divine life. You cannot kill it."

How might I acquire the kind of faith and joy the king's subject possessed?

The joy of heaven will begin as soon as we attain the character of heaven and do its duties. Theodore Parker

Fruit of Peace

During his first year in college,
Keith Miller was in a serious car accident.
For over an hour he lay with a broken neck,
waiting for an ambulance.

Closing his eyes, he began to pray.
As he did, a strange feeling of peace
came over him. He wrote later:

I remember lying beside the highway
and praying very simply.
I was very much awake. . . .
I thought to myself,

"What a shame to find out
that this kind of peace is a reality
so late in life."
For the first time I was not afraid to die.

I realized at that moment
that even in this tragedy . . .
there was something very personal [and] . . .
more important than anything else
I had ever known. The Taste of New Wine

Keith Miller's experience of peace
was a gift of the Holy Spirit.
John L. McKenzie describes it this way:

It is brought by Jesus
and is an achievement that is not possible
to the world. . . .
Peace comes through union with Jesus Christ

and surpasses all human thought;
it cannot be effected by human ingenuity.
Dictionary of the Bible

Even though we are helpless
to effect "spiritual" peace, we can become
instruments that God can use
to bring peace to our world.

End each meditation this week
with Saint Francis's beautiful "peace" prayer:

Lord,
make me an instrument of your peace.
Where there is hatred, let me sow love;
where there is injury, pardon;
where there is doubt, faith;
where there is despair, hope;
where there is darkness, light;
where there is sadness, joy.

Grant that I may not so much
seek to be consoled as to console;
to be understood as to understand;
to be loved as to love;
for it is in giving that we receive;
it is in pardoning that we are pardoned;
and it is in dying
that we are born into eternal life.

Peace is watching snow flutter down

Journal

*God does not want us to be in disorder
but in harmony and peace.*
1 Corinthians 14:33

Years ago a relative
gave author Christopher de Vinck
a little glass ball containing
a tiny snowman with a stovepipe hat.
When he turned the ball upside down
and shook it, a quiet snow fluttered down.
Softly and silently, it enveloped the snowman.
Christopher says the ball has been
on his desk for thirty years.
When disorder threatens his peace of mind,
he leans back against his chair,
picks up the glass ball, gives it a shake,
and watches the snow flutter down
around the snowman with the stovepipe hat.
Somehow it always works.
A quiet peace flutters down around him,
much as the quiet snow
flutters down around the snowman.

What helps me to dispose myself
to receive the gift of inner peace
that the Holy Spirit wishes to give us all?

*A contented mind
is the greatest blessing
a person can enjoy in this world.*
Joseph Addison

Journal

Peace is discerning the right decision

The peace that Christ gives
is to guide you in the decisions you make;
for it is to this peace
that God has called you. Colossians 3:15

Years ago Joe Paterno,
head football coach of Penn State,
was offered a "big money" contract
to coach the New England Patriots.
Ecstatic at the lucrative offer,
he prepared to meet the Patriot owner
in New York the next morning.
But that night he couldn't sleep.
He got up and paced the floor
no less than six times.
He was not at peace with his decision.
Finally, at 6:30 the next morning, he phoned
the Patriots and called off the meeting.
He explained that the opportunity
to impact the lives of college students
was more important than the money and
the prestige of being a pro coach.
With that phone call, a deep inner peace
fluttered down around the soul of Paterno.

Why is a lack of inner peace a good sign
that a decision is probably not of the Spirit?

Five great enemies of peace inhabit us:
avarice, ambition, envy, anger, and pride.
Petrarch

Peace is finding and reading a booklet

The LORD gives strength to his people and blesses them with peace. Psalms 29:11

RCL Publishing Company
received a handwritten letter.
It read:
"I am writing you concerning your booklet
Advent/Christmas 2000.
It was December 14, 1996,
that I was about to cross Racine Street
on the 60th side. I was heading west
to Steve's neighborhood store.
It was then I noticed one of your booklets
lying on the ground in a hole.
To make a long story short,
the next day, which was Sunday,
I began reading the booklet.
Suddenly, I began to feel real peaceful.
Just reading it made my mind at ease.
Now I want to know how I can get
other booklets similar to this one.
Yours truly, [Name withheld]."

How might I account for the person's
Feeling of peace in reading the booklet?

*From his cradle to his grave,
a man never does a single thing
which has any first or foremost object
save one—to secure peace of mind,
spiritual comfort, for himself.* Mark Twain

Peace is kneeling in prayer

Jesus said to his disciples,
"Peace is what I leave with you;
it is my own peace that I give you. . . .
Do not be worried and . . . afraid." John 14:27

Piri Thomas waited
until his young prison cell mate was asleep.
Then he knelt and prayed aloud to God.
When he finished, a voice added, "Amen!"
It was his young cell mate. "I believe
in *Dios,* also," said the kid. "Maybe you
don't believe it, but I used to go to church,
and I had the hand of God on me.
I felt always like you and I feel now . . .
quiet, peaceful." Then Piri asked the kid,
"What's it called, *chico,* this what we feel?"
"It's Grace by the Power of the Holy Spirit,"
the kid said. Piri writes: "I didn't ask any more.
There in the semi-darkness,
I found a new sense of awareness. . . .
I fell asleep thinking that I heard the kid
crying softly 'Cry, kid,' I thought,
'I hear even Christ cried.' "
Piri Thomas, *Down These Mean Streets*

When was the last time I prayed
with the fervor that Piri and the kid did?

Acquire inward peace,
and a multitude around you
will find their salvation. Saint Seraphim

Peace is seeking God's will

Journal

*Jesus said, "Jerusalem, Jerusalem! . . .
How many times I wanted to put my arms
around all your people . . .
but you would not let me!"* Luke 13:34

Kathryn Koob was one of 52 Americans
held hostage by Iran in the 1980s.
She says that
a remarkable source of strength
to help her deal with the trials of this time
came from these words of an old hymn:
"Have thine own way, Lord!
Have thine own way!
Thou are the potter; I am the clay.
Mold me and make me after thy will."
Kathryn said that these words gave her
not only a remarkable strength
to resign herself to God's will
but a profound "peace of mind."

Kathryn's attitude toward God's will
invites me to inventory my own attitude.
How attuned to God's will am I?
What keeps me from greater acceptance
of God's will, whatever it might bring?

*The earth is too small a star
and we too brief a visitor upon it
for anything to matter
more than the struggle for peace.*
Coleman McCarthy

Journal

Peace is doing what is right

To be controlled by the Spirit results in life and peace. Romans 8:6

The vast crowd in Washington
broke into a thunderous applause when
Lincoln arrived for his second inaugural.
It stunned him, because he'd gotten so used
to boos. No president in history had been
hated so bitterly as he had been,
because of the war and his stand on slavery.
The crowd grew deathly silent
when he began his address. It was an
amazing speech, ending with these words:
"With malice toward none; with charity
for all; with firmness in the right,
as God gives us to see the right, let us
strive on to finish the work we are in;
to bind up the nation's wounds;
to care for him who shall have borne
the battle, and for his widow and his orphan—
to do all which may achieve and cherish
a just and lasting peace among ourselves
and with all nations."

To what extent do I share Lincoln's
sentiments when it comes to our nation
and its deep prejudices and divisions?

*Lord, make me an instrument of your peace.
Where there is hatred, let me sow love.*
Saint Francis of Assisi

Peace is being controlled by the Spirit

*You, LORD, give perfect peace
to those who keep their purpose firm
and put their trust in you.* Isaiah 26:3

A young Jew fled the Nazis and went
to Chicago, where he met a Catholic girl.
One day a surprising question popped
into his mind: Could Jesus really be God?
He dismissed it, but it kept coming back.
He began to read about Jesus.
More importantly, he began to pray.
He writes: "I pleaded with God, 'Show me.' . . .
But God remained silent."
Then one evening something happened that
he found "almost impossible" to explain.
He writes: "A thought entered my mind. . . .
I use the term entered,
because it was not my own thought. . . .
It was unmistakable. It said, 'Of course,
Christ is God. How could you ever doubt it? . . .
Undoubtedly, this was the gift of Faith
I had read about. . . . I was filled
with a peace . . . I had never known before."
Paul Waldeman, *Richer Than a Millionaire*

What is the closest thing I've ever had to
the kind of experience the young man had?

*Peace is the evening star of the soul,
as virtue is its sun; and the two
are never far apart.* Charles Colton

111

Fruit of Patience

Anthony De Mello tells about a temple
that contained a thousand bells.
It was located on an island
that mysteriously disappeared in the sea.

Legend said that the bells continued to ring
from the sea, but you had to listen
attentively and patiently to hear them.

A young man journeyed to an island
not far from the island that disappeared.
He camped out all alone
on a deserted beach of the island.

After a week of patient listening,
he learned to block out the sea's roar
and listen only for the bells.
No bells sounded, however.

"Maybe the legend is false," he thought.
And so, after another week of listening,
he was tempted to give up.

The next day—his final day, he thought—
he lay on the beach as usual.
He had now grown accustomed
to the practice of listening
and did so with facility—even pleasure.

Suddenly
a deep, peaceful silence engulfed him.
It was then that he heard the tinkle
of a single bell, then another, then another,
then a thousand!

That lovely story leads us to
the "fruit of the Spirit," patience.

Commenting on the "fruits of the Spirit,"
theologians say that after we acquire
a facility in the practice of virtue,
we experience a "spiritual sweetness"
in practicing them. It is this "sweetness"
that we call a "fruit of the Spirit."

We might compare
the practice of virtue to roller-blading.
It is difficult—even unpleasant—at first.
We might even be tempted to give up,
as the young man in the story was.

But if we persevere
in the practice of virtue, the day will come
when a "spiritual sweetness" of the soul
will accompany it,
just as a "physical sweetness" of the body
accompanies roller-blading
when it is learned.

It is to the Holy Spirit's "fruit of patience"
that we now turn.

Patience is whistling a tune

Jesus said, "Martha, Martha!
You are worried and troubled
over so many things,
but just one is needed.
Mary has chosen the right thing." Luke 10:41–42

S. I. Hayakawa
writes in *Symbol, Status, and Personality:*
"Years ago I used to notice the difference
among motormen on the Indiana Avenue
streetcar line in Chicago—a street often
blocked by badly parked cars.
Some motormen would fly into a rage,
clang their bells, and shout incessantly
and furiously at drivers.
Other motormen would sit patiently,
whistling a tune or filling out a report."
In other words,
confronted with the same situation,
some motormen lived hellish lives
of anger and nervous tension;
other motormen lived tranquil lives
of peace and relaxation.

In which of the two groups of motormen
do I tend to find myself,
when I am confronted
with frustrating situations?

The world needs more warm hearts
and fewer hot heads. E. C. McKenzie

113

Patience is believing and trusting

[Jesus told this parable to teach us to pray patiently. A widow kept nagging a judge to help her. Finally he relented, saying,]
"Because of all the trouble this widow is giving me, I will see to it that she gets her rights." Luke 18:5

A Canadian woman sent the author this note: "On the 12th anniversary of my daughter's emotional illness, I asked Jesus to heal her as he did the woman who had hemorrhaged for 12 years. . . . I told Jesus I believed he could heal her after all those years and that I had enough faith for both of us. The next day I noticed the first small, positive signs pointing toward her recovery. They continued and each time our family saw them, we thanked Jesus, because we knew in our hearts he was answering our prayers. Now, six years later, she is a happy young woman. Even more beautiful, Jesus and the Holy Spirit are using her to help others."

Why do I think that God doesn't always answer people's prayers for a long while?

God answers prayers in his own time and in his own way, because only he knows how the answer will affect us and others.
From the Canadian woman's note

Patience is respecting God's timetable

*Be patient
and wait for the LORD to act. . . .
Don't give in to worry or anger;
it only leads to trouble. . . .
The LORD guides us
in the way we should go.* Psalms 37:7–8, 23

Little Zachary was a holy terror all day.
Finally his exasperated mother
reached the end of her patience.
She told him to sit down.
Then she ordered him to speak to God
about his behavior.
To her surprise, he complied calmly.
Then, after a little while,
he slowly got up out of the chair
and appeared remarkably repentant.
"Well, Zachary," asked his mother,
"Did God say
he was going to make you a better boy?"
"Yes," said Zachary, "but he also said
it might take longer than he expected."

A Chinese proverb says, "If you are patient
in one moment of anger, you will escape
a hundred days of sorrow." What is one thing
I can do to try to become more patient?

*Please be patient.
God is not yet finished with me.*
Words on a child's T-shirt

Patience is relaxing
in God's power

I waited patiently for the LORD'S help;
then he listened to me and heard my cry. . . .
He taught me to sing a new song. Psalms 40:1, 3

"As I write this, I'm at 35,000 feet. . . .
The airplane was an hour and a half late.
People are grumpy . . . downright mad.
Flight attendants are apologizing. . . .
The sports film on golf just broke down
and so did the nervous systems of
half the men on board. It's a zoo. . . .
For a change,
I refused to be hassled by today's delay.
I asked God to keep me calm and cheerful,
relaxed and refreshed.
Know what? He did. He really did!
No pills. No booze. . . .
Just relaxing in the power of Jesus."
Charles Swindoll, *Growing Strong in the Seasons of Life*

When was a time when I refused to be
hassled and simply relaxed in Jesus' power?

We must wait for God long and meekly—
in wind and wet,
in the lightning and the thunder,
in the cold and in the dark.
Wait, and he will come.
He never comes to those
who do not wait. Frederick W. Faber

Patience is giving birth to a dancing star

It is better to win control over yourself than over whole cities. Proverbs 16:32

In his book *The Finishing Touch,*
Charles Swindoll points out
the need for patience in helping people
to deal with their problems.
He says:
"You don't just force your way in.
Even if you've got the stuff that's needed . . .
even if you hold the piece perfectly shaped
to fit the other person's
missing part of the puzzle . . .
you can't push it into place.
You must not try. . . . You must wait.
Yes, that's correct. Wait. . . .
There are times (not always, but often)
when the better part of wisdom
restrains us from barging in
and trying to make someone accept help.
The time isn't right, so we wait."

What is one situation right now in my life
where God seems to be telling me to wait?

*Only those
who can contain within themselves
the pressure and chaos of tension
can give birth to a dancing star.*
Friedrich Wilhelm Nietzsche

Journal

Patience is waiting for a morning's wish

*See how patient farmers are
as they wait for their land
to produce precious crops.
They wait patiently
for the autumn and spring rains.
You also must be patient.
Keep your hopes high.*
James 5:7–8

"The sun is rising
on the morning of another day. . . .
What can I wish this day may bring me? . . .
A work to do that has real value. . . .
An understanding heart. . . .
A sense of humor and the power to laugh. . . .
The sense of God's presence.
And the patience
to wait for the coming of these things,
with the wisdom to know them
when they come, and the wit not to change
this morning wish of mine.
Walter Reid Hunt (source unknown)

Which of the above wishes
do I want more than all the others? Why?
What is one other wish I'd like to include?

*God makes a promise—
faith believes it, hope anticipates it,
patience quietly awaits it.*
E. C. McKenzie

Patience is listening to the inner voice

Encourage the timid, help the weak, be patient with everyone. 1 Thessalonians 5:14

Dan Begley settled into his plane seat
in Seattle, hoping to get a lot of work
done before arriving in Dallas.
Just then a mother and three kids got on.
The mother and a four-year-old sat
behind him; the two older kids, next to him.
Once airborne, they began turning around
every ten minutes to ask their mother,
"Where are we now?"
Dan's irritation rose to the "danger" level.
Suddenly an "inner voice" told him,
"Be patient! Love these kids. They need it."
He put away his work, took the in-flight
magazine, turned to the flight map, and
showed the kids the route to Dallas.
He divided the route into 15-minute lengths
so that they could see exactly where they
were at any moment. Then he explained
a lot of things about planes to them.
As the plane touched down in Dallas,
Dan asked if their father would be waiting.
A short silence ensued. Then one of the kids
said softly, "No! We buried him in Seattle."

How patient am I, especially with children?

Patience is bitter, but its fruit is sweet.
Jean Jacques Rousseau

Fruit of Kindness

Henry van Dyke wrote a short story
called "The Other Wise Man."
It is based on the gospel story of the magi
who followed the star to Bethlehem.
Van Dyke's story goes something like this.

A fourth "wise man," Artaban,
is scheduled to go with the other three.
He leaves his home to rendezvous with them.
On his person he carries a leather pouch
filled with precious gems, as a gift
for the newborn king whom he hopes to find.

On his way he meets someone in need
and stops to help them.
The delay causes him to miss the others,
and they leave without him.

Artaban travels on alone,
hoping to make up time and join them.
But, once again, he meets someone in need.
Again he helps the person.
This happens several more times.

To make a long story short,
Artaban never does join the other three.
Worse, he uses all his precious gems
to help needy people along the way.

Years pass and Artaban grows old.
He ends up penniless

in a faraway city called Jerusalem.
There he survives as a beggar.

One day he sees a criminal
being led off to execution.
He grows sad, because for some reason
he feels a close kinship with this man.
He wants to help him but can't.

When the criminal reaches the spot
where Artaban sits begging,
he turns to Artaban and says:

"Don't be sad, Artaban.
You have helped me all your life.
I was naked, and you clothed me.
I was sick, and you cared for me.
Yes, Artaban, you've helped me all your life."

Van Dyke's story introduces us to
the fifth fruit of the Holy Spirit: kindness.
Saint Paul spoke of its importance this way:

*You are the people of God. . . . You must
clothe yourselves with compassion,
kindness . . . and patience. . . .
And to all these qualities add love,
which binds all things together
in perfect unity.* Colossians 3:12, 14

And so it is to the "fruit of kindness"
that we now turn.

Kindness is using honey, not vinegar

The LORD gave this message to Zechariah:
"Long ago I gave these commands
to my people:
'You must . . . show kindness and mercy
to one another.' " Zechariah 7:8–9

President Franklin Roosevelt
needed every vote he could get to pass
an important bill before the Senate.
He studied the list of senators
who opposed the bill
but might be persuaded to reconsider.
He discovered that one—like himself—
was a stamp collector.
The night before the bill was to be voted on,
he spread out his own collection on a table,
phoned the senator, and asked him
to come to the White House to advise him
on something pertaining to it.
The senator was absolutely thrilled.
The next day the senator voted for the bill.
Although FDR's kindness
was politically motivated, it illustrates
an important point: You can catch more flies
with honey than with vinegar.

What keeps me from being kind to people?

One of the hardest things to give away
is kindness. It usually always
comes back to you. Anonymous

Kindness is listening to the heart

*"I beg you to be kind
and listen to our brief account."* Acts 24:4

Erma was waiting for her flight.
It felt good just sitting and
reading a book, with no one to bother her.
Just then a woman sat down and said,
"Bet it's cold in Chicago." Erma said coldly,
"Probably." The woman kept talking,
and Erma kept responding coldly.
Then the woman dropped the bombshell.
She was taking her husband back to Chicago.
He had died after 53 years of marriage.
Erma's heart sank. She closed her book,
held the woman's hand, and listened.
When the call to board came, they walked
arm in arm to the plane.
Then they went to their assigned seats,
which were a few rows apart.
As Erma buckled up, she heard
the woman say to the person next to her,
"Bet it's cold in Chicago."
Erma found herself praying: "Dear God,
help the person next to her listen kindly."

Who is one person who needs kindness?
What keeps me from extending it?

*I'm going your way,
so let us go hand in hand. . . . Let us help
one another while we may.* William Morris

Kindness is chatting with a freezing boy

Journal

*The Spirit
is God's mark of ownership on you. . . .
Get rid of all bitterness. . . .
No more hateful feelings of any sort.
Instead, be kind and tenderhearted
to one another.* Ephesians 4:30–32

Henry Ward Beecher
was a 19th-century Congregational minister.
He was an outspoken opponent of slavery
and an early advocate of women's rights.
One cold day he stopped to buy a newspaper
from a shabbily dressed youngster
who was visibly shivering on a street corner.
"Son!" said the compassionate Beecher,
"you're actually freezing out here."
Demonstrating a maturity beyond his years,
the youngster said, "I was, mister,
until you stopped to talk with me and buy
one of my papers."

What kindness by another
warmed my heart recently?
What kindness by me
warmed another's heart?

*So many gods, so many creeds,
So many paths that wind and wind,
While just the art of being kind
Is all the sad world needs.*
Ella Wheeler Wilcox

Journal

Kindness is passing it on

Kind words bring life, but cruel words crush your spirit. Proverbs 15:4

Chris Zorich lived alone with his mother in a bad section of Chicago. He beat the odds, went to Notre Dame, won the Orange Bowl MVP trophy, and was drafted by the Chicago Bears. *Inside Sports* said, "Zorich's training schedule can accurately be described as religious. He begins each day by stopping in at church." The magazine adds that this is part of the Zorich paradox. On the field, his play mirrors the harshness of his neighborhood life. Off the field, his life mirrors the kindness of his home life. He helps throwaway kids and on Mother's Day distributes corsages at a shelter for battered women.

What is one difficult hurdle that the Spirit has helped me overcome in my life?

Have you had a kindness shown?
Pass it on;
'Twas not given for thee alone,
Pass it on;
Let it travel down the years,
Let it wipe another's tears,
'Till in Heaven the deed appears—
Pass it on. Henry Burton, "Pass It On"

Kindness is finding and praising the good

*Let other people praise you . . . ;
never do it yourself.* Proverbs 27:2

Roots was the most watched
TV miniseries in broadcast history.
It grew out of Alex Haley's search
for his African heritage. Haley once said
that a guiding principle in his life came
from a bumper sticker that he saw in his
youth. It read: "Find the good and praise it!"
One day
Lyndon Johnson was praised lavishly
during the introduction to an address
to Baylor University students. He began,
"This is a moment I deeply wish my parents
could have lived to share.
My father would have enjoyed what you have
so generously said of me, and my mother
would have believed every word of it."

Albert Schweitzer once said,
"Constant kindness can accomplish much.
As the sun melts ice, kindness melts
misunderstanding, mistrust, and hostility."
To what extent is it a guiding principle
in my life to praise the good I find
rather than complain about the evil I see?

*Kind words can be short and easy to speak,
but their echoes are truly endless.*
Mother Teresa

Journal

_____

_____

_____

_____

_____

_____

_____

_____

_____

_____

_____

_____

_____

Kindness is joining the golden chain

"May the LORD deal kindly with you, as you have dealt . . . with me."
Ruth 1:8 (NRSV)

Billy Graham tells the story of Paul Haley, a six-year-old boy from Denver. Paul was dying of terminal cancer and had expressed the desire to see the president of the United States before he died. President Eisenhower was vacationing in Denver at the time. He learned of Paul's desire and decided to surprise him. On Sunday morning the president ordered his limousine to be chauffeured to the Haley home. He went to the door himself. When the Haleys saw who it was, they were overwhelmed. Years later they, their neighbors, and thousands of people were still talking about the act of kindness that the busy president performed for a dying boy.

What is one act of kindness I went out of my way to bestow on another?

Kindness is the golden chain by which society is bound together.
Johann von Goethe

Kindness is discovering wisdom

You must all have the same attitude . . . ;
love one another, and be kind. 1 Peter 3:8

" 'What is real good?'
I asked in a musing mood:
'Order,' said the law court;
'Knowledge,' said the school;
'Truth,' said the wise man;
'Pleasure,' said the fool;
'Love,' said the maiden;
'Beauty,' said the page;
'Freedom,' said the dreamer;
'Home,' said the sage;
'Fame,' said the soldier;
'Equity,' said the seer—
Spake my heart full sadly:
'The answer is not here';
Then, within my bosom, softly, this I heard:
'Each heart holds the secret—
Kindness is the word.' " John Boyle O'Reilly

How do I understand this Chinese proverb:
"Better to be kind at home
than to burn incense in a distant place?"
What keeps me from being kinder at home?

Kindness
is more important than wisdom,
and the recognition of this
is the beginning of wisdom. Theodore Isaac Rubin

Fruit of Generosity

A Guy Named Joe
is a movie about a military fighter pilot
played by Spencer Tracy.
He has many admirable qualities,
but he also has a serious selfish streak.

To make things more complicated,
he is losing his combat edge and nearing
the end of his fighting days.
The woman who loves him realizes all this
and wants him to apply for
a noncombatant flying status.

To make a long story short,
Joe decides to fly one more mission.
Tragically, he is killed when he heroically
dives his fighter plane
into a Nazi aircraft carrier.

Joe wakes up in the next world, in a place
midway between heaven and hell.
He is assigned the job of being
a kind of guardian angel to new pilots.

In the course of his assignment,
his selfishness slowly gives way
to a beautiful generosity.
It allows him to put other people's needs
ahead of his own personal desires.
When this happens,
he is welcomed into heaven.

A Guy Named Joe introduces us
to the fruit of the Spirit that Paul calls
"generosity" or goodness. Galatians 5:22
Someone said of "giving:"

The one thing that we can all give is:
sincere forgiveness to our enemies,
patient tolerance to our opponents,
good example to our children,
healthy respect to ourselves,
loving fidelity to our spouses, and
a helping hand to all in need.

And Robert Rodenmayer reminds us that
there are three kinds of giving:
"grudge-giving,"
"duty-giving," and
"thanks-giving."

Grudge-giving says, "I hate to give to you;"
duty-giving says, "I ought to give to you;"
thanks-giving says, "I want to give to you."

This week's meditations
focus on the "fruit of generosity."
It empowers us not only to give to people
according to their special needs
but also to give with genuine joy.

Generosity is giving from the heart

Journal

Jesus said,
"Give to others, and God will give to you. . . .
The measure you use for others is the one
that God will use for you." Luke 6:38

John D. Rockefeller's obituary read:
"He died this morning [May 23, 1937]
missing the century mark
by little more than two years.
The richest man
in the world was also the greatest giver."
Chronicles of the 20th Century

But that was not always the case.
Beginning with little formal education
and less capital, Rockefeller got into
the oil business. At the age of 53,
he was incredibly rich and world famous.
He was also troubled and disillusioned.
Success hadn't brought happiness.
Then came a life-changing decision.
After deep soul-searching,
he resolved to use his wealth to help others.
He established a foundation
and dedicated it
to fighting disease and ignorance.

What keeps me from giving more than I do?

One reason there are so many dollar bills
in the church collection basket
is that there is no smaller bill. Anonymous

Journal

Generosity is giving to Jesus

Jesus said, "Whenever you refused to help one of these least important ones, you refused to help me." Matthew 25:45

Malcolm Kushner tells about a chairman of a hospital fund drive who learned that the richest tycoon in town hadn't yet made a contribution. Calling on him, he said, "Our records show you've not yet donated to our drive. The tycoon said, "And do your records show my mother died penniless? Do they show that my brother is disabled? Do they show that my sister was abandoned and left to support four kids?"
The chairman felt ashamed of his approach. He apologized, "No, they don't. I'm sorry."
"Well," said the tycoon, "if I didn't help my own family, why should I help you?"
The Light Touch: How to Use Humor for Business Success

Someone said, "We laugh at that story, but isn't it a true picture of our society's attitude toward the needy of our human family?" Why do/don't I agree?

Suppose there are brothers or sisters who need clothes and don't have enough to eat. What good is there in your saying to them, "God bless you! Keep warm and eat well!"—if you don't give them the necessities of life? James 2:15–16

Generosity is giving the best thing

Jesus said,
"If one of you wants to be great,
you must be the servant of the rest . . .
For even the Son of Man
did not come to be served."
Mark 10:43, 45

In his book *The Greatest Thing in the World,*
Henry Drummond says:
"There is no happiness in having or getting,
but only in giving.
Half of the world is on the wrong scent
in the pursuit of happiness.
They think it consists in having and getting,
and being served by others.
It consists in giving and serving others."

When was the last time
that I gave generously, enthusiastically,
and from the heart?

The best thing
to give an enemy is forgiveness;
to an opponent, tolerance;
to a friend, your heart;
to your child, a good example;
to your father, deference;
to your mother, conduct that will
make her proud of you;
to yourself, respect; to all, charity.
Francis M. Balfour

Journal

Generosity is not counting the cost

Jesus said, "The Son of Man . . . came to serve and to give his life to redeem many people." Mark 10:45

Lafcadio Hearn tells the story
of a Chinese farmer who lived on a hilltop.
One day the farmer happened to glance out
to sea. What he saw made his heart tremble.
A great tidal wave had developed
and was building up a momentum
that would sweep away his neighbors
who were at work in the lowlands.
Without the slightest hesitation
he put a match to his rice ricks
and rang the temple bell furiously.
His neighbors looked up
and saw the blaze on the hilltop.
Thinking the farmer's house was on fire,
they rushed up the hill to help him.
Minutes later, safely atop the hill,
they saw the tidal wave sweep through
the lowland fields they had just left.
They realized "their salvation and its cost."

What can I do to prepare myself
to act in an emergency with the same kind
of generosity as the hilltop farmer did?

*Great occasions
do not make heroes or cowards.
They simply unveil them.* W. B. Prescott

Generosity is doing whatever I can do

*Jesus saw a very poor widow dropping in
[the Temple treasury] two little copper coins.
He said, "I tell you that this poor widow
put in more than all the others. . . .
She . . . gave all she had to live on."* Luke 21:2–4

Journalist Leo Aikman said there are
four kinds of "bones" in every organization.
First, there are the Wishbones.
They see the problem, talk about it, and hope
that someone will do something about it.
Second, there are the Jawbones.
They see the problem, talk about it,
talk about it some more, but do little else.
Third, there are the Knucklebones.
They see the problem, talk about it,
and criticize what's being done about it.
Finally, there are the Backbones.
They see the problem, study it prayerfully,
roll up their sleeves,
and do what needs to be done.

On a scale of one (low) to ten (high),
How closely do I resemble the following:
Wishbone, Jawbone, Knucklebone, Backbone?

*There comes a time
when one must take a position
that is neither safe, politic, nor popular,
but one must take it because it is right.*
Martin Luther King Jr.

Journal

Generosity is putting in my share

"There is more happiness in giving than in receiving." Acts 20:35

The film *The Bishop's Wife* created a stir years ago. It concerned an Episcopal bishop who was missing life's point because of his dream to build a magnificent cathedral. God sent an angel to straighten him out. The film ends with the angel writing the bishop's Christmas homily. It reads: "Once upon a midnight clear, there was a child's cry. A blazing star hung over a stable and wise men came with gifts. . . . We celebrate it with stars on Christmas trees . . . but especially with gifts. . . . [But we've] forgotten to hang up the stocking for the child born in a manger. It is his birthday we're celebrating. Don't let us forget that. Let us ask ourselves what we would wish for most, and then let each put in his share. Loving kindness, warm hearts, and a stretched-out hand of tolerance."

What do I wish for most—and, therefore, what should I put into the child's stocking?

Help us to reach beyond our own comforts, beyond our own ambitions and satisfactions, to a larger world. Richard Ferris

Generosity is giving with dignity

Journal

*"Each man is to bring a gift as he is able,
in proportion to the blessings
that the LORD your God has given him."*
Deuteronomy 16:16–17

Grace Willard and her husband
were driving in a rural area through snow
in near-zero weather.
Suddenly they came upon a Native American
woman holding a baby in her arms.
Her husband had deserted her,
and she was trying to hitchhike 400 miles
to live with a relative.
They took the mother and child home,
warmed them, fed them, and then called
a young Native American pastor to go
with them as they drove her to the relative.
The relative was clearly a poor man,
but he insisted on giving them something
for bringing her all that distance.
They refused, until the Native American
pastor took Grace's husband aside
and explained that the relative
needed to give it for his own sake.

What was a recent act of generosity
that I did? That someone did for me?

*I'd rather be a beggar and give my last
dollar like a king than be a king and spend
my money like a beggar.* Robert Ingersoll

Fruit of Faithfulness

Henry Francis Lyte was an old man.
His health was broken—but not his spirit.
Those who were present at his last sermon
in Lower Brixham, England,
report that he could barely mount the pulpit.

One day he was sitting in his study.
He picked up his King James Bible and began
to read the story of Jesus' appearance
to the two disciples on the road to Emmaus.

He came to the part where they
arrive at their home in Emmaus with Jesus
(they still didn't recognize him).
When Jesus made as if he was going further,
they said:

*"Abide with us: for it is toward evening,
and the day is far spent." And he went in
to tarry with them.* Luke 24:29)

Suddenly Lyte's heart began to burn
within him—
as the hearts of the two disciples did
as they listened to Jesus on the road.

Lyte picked up his quill and hastily
began to write on a piece of paper.
When he finished, the paper contained
one of history's most inspiring hymns:

*Abide with me; fast falls the eventide;
The darkness deepens; Lord, with me abide;*

*When other helpers fail, and comforts flee,
Help of the helpless, O abide with me.*

*Swift to its close
ebbs out life's little day;
Earth's joys grow dim, its glories pass away;
Change and decay in all around I see;
O Thou who changest not, abide with me.*

Not long afterward, Lyte was dead.
But the words live on.

They are the words of a man
who stayed *faithful* to his Lord.
And in return, the Lord's Spirit filled him
with a glow that made all the struggles
of life count as nothing.

This week's meditations focus on
the fruit of the Holy Spirit
that Paul calls "faithfulness."

It is the kind of faithfulness
that inspired Lyte to pen "Abide with Me."
It is the kind of faithfulness
that inspires others to stay faithful, also.

Faithfulness is
staying the course

*Do not be surprised at the painful test
you are suffering. . . . Rather be glad
that you are sharing Christ's sufferings,
so that you may be full of joy
when his glory is revealed.* 1 Peter 4:12–13

A Belgium doctor invited nurse Edith Cavell
to set up a medical clinic in Brussels.
When war came in 1914, she secretly treated
and helped 200 Allied soldiers to escape.
The Germans found out and
sentenced her to death.
A chaplain describes her last moments:
"We partook of Holy Communion together.
At the close of the little service,
I began to repeat the words, 'Abide with me,'
and she joined. . . . Then I said good-bye. . . .
She smiled and said, 'We shall meet again.'"
When the British ship *Stella*
was sinking with 105 victims still on it,
a woman stood on the bridge and sang
"Abide with Me." Immediately the others
joined in, remaining faithful to their Lord
to the end.

Why do I think "Abide with Me" has such
power to inspire and strengthen people?

*Just over the hill is a beautiful valley,
but you must climb the hill to see it.*
E. C. McKenzie

Journal

Faithfulness is tending God's lamp daily

I . . . forget what is behind me and do my best to reach what is ahead. Philippians 3:13

"Faithfulness is consecration in overalls.
It is the steady acceptance and performance
of the . . . immediate task . . .
because it is there to be done and so
is a manifestation of the will of God.
Faithfulness
means continuing quietly with the job
we have been given . . . not yielding
to the restless desire for change.
It means tending the lamp quietly for God
without wondering
how much longer it has to go on. . . .
A lot of the road to heaven
has to be taken at thirty miles per hour."
Evelyn Underhill, *The Fruits of the Spirit*

What motivates me to keep tending
the lamp of God day in and day out?

Were a star quenched on high,
For ages would its light,
Still traveling downward from the sky,
Shine on our mortal sight. //
So when a great man dies,
For years beyond our ken,
The light he leaves behind him lies
Upon the paths of men.
Henry Wadsworth Longfellow

Faithfulness is renewing myself daily

[One day Jesus said to his disciples,]
"Let us go off by ourselves
to some place where we will be alone
and you can rest a while." So they started
out in a boat . . . to a lonely place. Mark 6:31–32

John A. Sanford wrote in *Soul Journey:*
"When an Apache woman gave birth
to her child, she did so under a tree."
Later in life if the child
experienced a need for spiritual renewal,
it made a pilgrimage back to the tree,
performed a spiritual ceremony, and left
spiritually strengthened and renewed.

The sensitivity and fidelity of Apaches
to spiritual renewal invites me to inventory
my own sensitivity and fidelity
to the Spirit's invitation for me
to undergo a periodic spiritual renewal.
How can I tell if the Spirit might be
inviting me to such a renewal? What are
some ways I might go about the renewal?

I cannot overstate the importance
of the habit of quiet meditation
for health of body, mind, and spirit.
Modern man's life is grossly abnormal. . . .
We need to explore our lives . . .
quietly and unhurried in his presence.
Dr. W. R. Luxton

Faithfulness is emulating what Mary did

Simeon . . . said to Mary, . . .
"This child . . . will be a sign from God
which many people will speak against. . . .
And sorrow, like a sharp sword,
will break your own heart." Luke 2:34–35

Simeon's prophecy gave rise
to Mary's title "Our Lady of Sorrows."
Tradition lists seven major sorrows:
Simeon's prophecy at the presentation of
Jesus; the flight of the Holy Family into
Egypt; the loss of Jesus in the Temple,
the carrying of the cross by Jesus,
the crucifixion of Jesus on Calvary;
the removal of Jesus from the cross,
the burial of Jesus.
The feast of Our Lady of Sorrows
dates from the 15th century.
The hymn *(Stabat Mater)*,
written for the feast, reads in part:
"At the cross her station keeping,
Stood the mournful Mother weeping,
Close to Jesus to the last . . .
Now at length the sword has passed."

With what faithfulness do I follow Jesus?

Count that day lost whose low
descending sun views from the hand
no worthy action done. Author unknown

Journal

Faithfulness is
tapping into God's power

I have learned this secret, so that
anywhere, at any time . . .
I have the strength to face all conditions
by the power that Christ gives me.
Philippians 4:12–13

Joe Mattison is a surgeon and a minister.
In a speech to Princeton alumni,
he cited a survey that showed
only one in five people felt
that sickness brings out the best in us.
A surgical colleague of Mattison says
that one reason why this may be true is
contained in Bishop Wescott's observation:
"Great occasions
do not make heroes or cowards.
They simply unveil them. . . .
Silently and imperceptibly, as we wake
or sleep, we grow strong or weak,
and at last some crisis
shows us what we have become."

What is Wescott's point, and how does it
explain why sickness may not always
bring out the best in us?
How faithfully do I try to live my faith
in every phase of my life—seen and unseen?

Character
may be manifested in great moments,
but it is made in small ones. Phillips Brooks

Journal

Faithfulness is becoming myself

*"Well done. . . . You have been faithful
in managing small amounts,
so I will put you in charge of large amounts."*
Matthew 25:21

A man died and met Peter in heaven.
Soon they were conversing enthusiastically.
Aware that Peter had a lot of
inside information, the man said,
"I'm a military history buff. Tell me,
who was the greatest general in history?"
Pointing to someone nearby, Peter said,
"That's him!" The man was shocked, saying,
"There must be a mistake. I knew that man
on earth; he was just a day laborer."
"Yes," said Peter, "but had he developed
his potential, he would have been
history's greatest general."
Psychologist Abraham Maslow says,
"If you deliberately plan to be less
than you are capable of being,
then, I warn you that you'll be unhappy
for the rest of your life.
You'll be evading your own . . . possibilities."

How well am I becoming myself?

*To be what we are
and to become what we are capable of being
is the only end of life.*
Robert Louis Stevenson

Faithfulness is living in God's presence

Journal

*"Be faithful to me . . .
and I will give you life
as your prize of victory."* Revelation 2:10

James Kavanaugh
tells the story of an Italian couple
who operate a neighborhood grocery store.
Although they don't talk a lot about God,
they live in his presence.
Their love for each other makes their store
a holy place. Kavanaugh says,
"When I leave the store, I somehow feel
more human . . . closer to God."
Finally,
after a twelve-hour day, the couple
put things in order for the next day,
turn off the lights, and bolt the door.
"Then they go home, have a glass of wine,
and watch TV and say their simple prayers
to a friendly God
or light a candle to their madonna.
Sometimes they play cards or reminisce.
Then they go to bed."
God Lives . . . From Religious Fear to Spiritual Freedom

What is so holy
about the way the couple live.
How similarly to them do I live?

*God has not called me to be successful;
he has called me to be faithful.* Mother Teresa

Fruit of Gentleness

Frederick Buechner
was parked by the side of the road.
He was deeply depressed
and concerned about a family situation.
Suddenly, out of nowhere came a car.

For some reason,
Buechner's eyes were drawn
not to the driver of the car
but to the license plate on it.
He couldn't believe what he saw.
The plate contained just one word: *trust*.

When Buechner recovered
from the impact of what had just happened,
he wondered,
"Was it a mere coincidence?
Was it a word from God?
Or was it a little bit of both?"

Later he happened to mention the incident
in one of his books.
Then one day he got a visit
from the trust officer of a bank.
The officer had read his description
of the incident
and brought him the license plate.
It now sits on Buechner's bookshelf.
Retold from Buechner's *Telling Secrets*

Regardless of what you say
about the car incident, one thing is for sure.

It is with this kind of gentleness
that the Holy Spirit usually acts
in our lives.

And it is this kind of visitation
from the Holy Spirit that inspires us
to want to bless those around us
in a similar way.

This week's meditations
focus on gentleness and the joy and peace
it brings into our lives—
whether we are the giver or receiver
of the blessing.

Consider ending each meditation
with this lovely passage
atttributed to Stephen Grellet:

*I shall pass
through this world but once.
Any good that I can do, or any kindness
that I can show to any human being,
let me do it now and not defer it.
For I shall not pass this way again.*
(slightly adapted)

Gentleness is serving others quietly

Journal

[The wine ran out at a wedding.
Jesus said to the servants,]
"Fill these jars with water."
They filled them . . . and then he told them,
"Now . . . take it to the man in charge. . . ."
He tasted it . . . and said . . . ,
"Everyone else serves the best wine first . . .
But you have kept the best wine
until now!" John 2:7–10

There's something beautifully gentle
about Jesus as he quietly changes water
to wine for two young newlyweds
who badly underestimated
the celebrating capacity of their guests.
To borrow a phrase from William Barclay,
it is this kind of "divine courtesy"
that makes Jesus so approachable.

How do I understand
the phrase the "divine courtesy" of Jesus?
How might I imitate it—perhaps today?

A good marriage
is not a contract between two persons
but a sacred covenant between three.
Too often Christ is never invited
to the wedding. . . . Why?
It is because we have misrepresented him
and forgotten his joyful outlook on life.
Donald T. Kauffman

Journal

Gentleness is living simply and humbly

Jesus said, "Take my yoke and put it on you, and learn from me, because I am gentle and humble in spirit."
Matthew 11:29

Robert Bellarmine was so small that
he used to stand on a stool to preach.
Spiritually, however, he was a giant.
Born in Italy in the wake of the Protestant
Reformation, he worked tirelessly
to keep the Church from fracturing.
He lectured with such clarity and honesty
that even Protestants came to hear him.
His writings ranged
from complex theological tracts
to simple catechisms
(one was translated into 62 languages).
After being made a cardinal
—over his protests—
he never lost his humble simplicity.
He ate what the poor ate and sold
the tapestries of his "cardinal's apartment"
to "clothe the naked," observing,
"The walls can't catch cold."

How well do I reflect in my life
Jesus' teaching to be gentle and humble?

*The greatest truths are the simplest;
and so are the greatest people.*
Augustus and Julius Hare

Gentleness is being like my child

*You must be kind toward all,
a good and patient teacher,
who is gentle.* 2 Timothy 2:24–25

"Last night my little boy confessed to me
Some childish wrong;
And kneeling at my knee,
He prayed with tears—
'Dear God, make me a man
Like Daddy—wise and strong;
I know You can.' //
Then while he slept
I knelt beside his bed,
Confessed my sins,
And prayed with low-bowed head.
'O God, make me a child
Like my child here—
Pure, guileless,
Trusting Thee with faith sincere.' "
Andrew Gillies

What keeps me from being more gentle
and tenderhearted toward others—
especially those closest to me?

An anonymous wife prayed
for her husband:

*Lord, place your hand on his shoulder.
Whisper your voice in his ear.
Put your love in his heart.
Help him fulfill your plan in life.*

Journal

Gentleness is being like a kind cardinal

"He will not argue or shout. . . .
He will not break off a bent reed,
nor put out a flickering lamp."
Matthew 12:19–20

Someone described Cardinal Bernardin as "the kindest, gentlest man I ever knew." Thousands of people in Chicago agreed. The front-page story of his burial described how people stood in the cold, waiting, in some cases, for half a day and three deep. "An eerie, respectful silence followed the cortege as it snaked through the city. . . . People held signs, lit candles, rang bells and held pictures. At Wabash Avenue and Randolph Street, a roller blader in skin-tight purple and yellow jumpsuit stood with head bowed, hands in prayer. . . . A boy in a blue winter jacket held up a sign he had colored on a sheet of orange paper. "Bye, Joe," it said. "You have everlasting life." Chicago Tribune (Nov. 21, 1996)

Cardinal Bernardin practiced what Fredrick W. Faber preached years ago: "Kindness has converted more sinners than zeal, eloquence and learning." Why am I not gentler toward people, especially sinners (people I don't like)?

Feelings are everywhere—be gentle. J. Masai

Gentleness is helping another grow wings

"If anyone hits you on one cheek,
let him hit the other one too. . . .
Do for others just what you want them
to do for you." Luke 6:29, 31

The following is written from the viewpoint
of a young person to an adult:
"Each time
you're kind and gentle and encouraging,
each time you try to understand
because you really care,
my heart grows wings. . . .
I want you to know that.
I want you to know
how important you are to me.
How you can be the creator of the person
that is me, if you choose. Please choose. . . .
It will not be easy for you. . . .
The nearer you approach,
the blinder I might strike back. . . .
I fight against the very thing I cry out for.
But I am told that love is stronger
than the strongest walls,
and in this lies my hope. My only hope."
Author unknown

How might I put into practice
the above words, right now in my life?

Kindness is loving people
more than they deserve. Joseph Joubert

Journal

Gentleness is seeing as God sees

Your beauty should consist of . . .
the ageless beauty
of a gentle and quiet spirit. 1 Peter 3:4

The gentle person is not someone
crippled with an inferiority complex.
On the contrary, the gentle person
is someone who has stopped being fooled
about himself and has accepted
God's estimate of his own life.
"He knows he is as weak and helpless
as God has declared him to be,
but paradoxically,
he knows at the same time that he is
in the sight of God
of more importance than angels.
In himself, nothing; in God, everything.
That is his motto.
He knows well that the world
will never see him as God sees him
and he has stopped caring. . . .
He will be patient to wait for the day
when everything will get its own price tag
and real worth will . . . shine forth
in the Kingdom of their Father."
A. W. Tozer, *The Pursuit of God*

How closely does this description fit me?

Power can do by gentleness
what violence fails to accomplish. Claudian

Gentleness is living as Jesus lived

"Forgive us the wrongs we have done, as we forgive the wrongs that others have done to us." Matthew 6:12

Richard Weaver was a British coal miner, a semipro boxer, and a heavy drinker. He underwent a remarkable conversion and became a deeply loved evangelist. Shortly after turning his life over to Jesus, he came upon an older miner trying to take a coal wagon, by force, from a boy miner. He describes what then happened: "I said to him, 'Tom, you mustn't take that wagon.' He swore and . . . struck me . . . five times. I turned my cheek for the sixth stroke; but he turned away, cursing. I shouted after him, 'The Lord forgive you, for I do, and the Lord save you.' "
The next morning, Richard went, as usual, into the mine. He writes:
"Tom was the first man I saw. . . . When I came to him he burst into tears. . . . I gave him my hand, and we went each to his work." William James
in *Freedom, Love and Truth*, compiled by William Inge

How ready am I to do what Richard did?

There is only one way to be a gentleman— but there are hundreds of ways not to be.
E. C. McKenzie

Fruit of Self-control

A Sioux Indian prayer reads:
O Great Spirit,
Whose voice I hear in the winds . . .
I need your strength. . . .
I seek strength,
not to be greater than my brother,
but to fight my greatest enemy—myself.

Self-control is an ongoing struggle.
It begins the day we are born and,
normally, moves through three stages:
self-centeredness, other-centeredness, and
God-centeredness.

During the self-centered stage, our focus is,
primarily, on ourselves and our own enjoyment.
We want to be free to do as we please.
We don't realize, however, that at this stage
we are anything but free.
We are slaves to ourselves.
If we remain in this stage,
we are doomed to unhappiness—
chasing one fleeting pleasure after another.

We move to the next stage when we begin
to shift the focus away from ourselves.
We do this by assuming social obligations,
like friendships and commitments.
Assuming these responsibilities
is a giant leap forward toward self-control.

We move to the final stage
when we become aware of
our spiritual *identity* and *destiny*
(God's children called to share God's life).
What God said to Moses,
God says, in effect, to every human being:

"I am now giving you the choice
between life and death . . .
and I call heaven and earth to witness
the choice you make. Choose life." Deuteronomy 30:19

At this stage, we begin to relate personally
to God as Father, Jesus as Brother, and
the Holy Spirit as our constant Companion.
We begin to see that Christian life
is a personal response to God's invitation
to "choose life." Saint Paul sums up
our Christian calling this way:

God poured out the Holy Spirit
abundantly on us
through Jesus Christ our Savior,
so that by his grace
we might be put right with God
and come into possession
of the eternal life we hope for. Titus 3:6–7

What I say is this:
let the Spirit direct your lives. . . .
The Spirit has given us life;
He must also control our lives. Galatians 5:16, 25

Self-control is ignoring "silly tollbooths"

*Do not let evil defeat you;
instead, conquer evil with good.* Romans 12:21

Mel Brooks's film *Blazing Saddles* is a spoof
on westerns. In one scene the bad guys are pursuing the good guys. To slow down
the bad guys, the good guys hit upon
a "clever" strategy. They erect a "nickel"
tollbooth across the escape route.
The strategy works.
The bad guys don't have enough nickels.
So they wait while one of their number
gallops back to town to get more nickels.
Meanwhile, the good guys ride off to safety.
A human potential expert, Glenn Van Ekeren
observes, "How ridiculous! . . . Anyone
realizes how easy it would be for the bad
guys to ride around this silly tollbooth."
Then he notes that our behavior toward
obstacles in life resembles the behavior
of the bad guys to the "silly tollbooth"
in *Blazing Saddles.*

What Van Ekeren says about our behavior
toward life's "silly tollbooths" holds true
for our "spiritual" life as well. What "silly
tollbooth" is hindering my spiritual growth?

*Knowing the truth and not doing it
is as foolish as writing a love letter
and not mailing it.* Anonymous

Journal

Self-control is monitoring vulnerability

I may be able to speak the languages
of human beings and even of angels . . .
I may have all knowledge
and understand all secrets . . .
but if I have no love . . .
this does me no good. 1 Corinthians 13:1–3

Today we try to dismiss
the era of Nazi concentration camps
as an "era of madness" in history.
Yet those responsible for this insanity
could all read and write eloquently.
They could speak many languages.
They understood the secrets of science.
Their cities were engineering masterpieces
complete with modern parks and
schools of art and music.
Their culture was the envy of Europe.
There were, in many ways, like us.

How do I explain this "era of madness"
coming from such a sophisticated culture?
What evidence suggests it could happen
in our own sophisticated culture?

I have one great fear in my heart
that one day
when they are turned to loving,
they will find we are turned to hating.
A black preacher speaking of the white culture
in Alan Paton's *Cry, the Beloved Country*

Self-control is digging up "rocks"

[Jesus said of his disciples' failure to stay awake and pray,] "The spirit is willing, but the flesh is weak." Mark 14:38

There's an old story about a farmer who was perennially plagued by a large rock located in the center of his field. Apart from the inconvenience of plowing around it each year, he sometimes forgot it and damaged equipment on it. He swore that he would take time off some day and dig it out once and for all. But he kept putting it off year after year. One day he decided to act. To his surprise, the rock was almost totally on the surface and quite easily removed. He thought to himself, "Why did it take me so long to get around to digging it up? How much grief I could have saved myself had I removed it right away!"

Someone said, "The field of life is full of 'rocks' like the one in the farmer's field. Why do we procrastinate in removing them?" What is such a "rock" that is causing me undue anxiety and aggravation?

Work as though everything depends on you; pray as though everything depends on God. Attributed to Ignatius of Loyola

Journal

Self-control is avoiding mosquitoes

[Jesus asked a Samaritan woman for a drink. She answered,] "You are a Jew, and I am a Samaritan—so how can you ask me for a drink?" (Jews will not use the same cups and bowls that Samaritans use.) John 4:9

David Feldman's *Do Penguins Have Knees?* answers such questions as, "Why don't we feel a mosquito bite until it begins to itch?" Feldman says the mosquito is so light and its biting technique so skillful that we don't feel it—even though the biting process lasts about a minute. The mosquito's technique includes exuding a saliva that anesthetizes the person bitten and lubricating the bite. Only after the anesthetic wears off are we aware the bite took place. Acquiring a prejudice is not unlike acquiring a mosquito bite. Only after the process is complete do we realize that it ever took place.

What is one prejudice I have? How am I trying to control it?

One of the noblest pleasures in life is to discover a new truth, and the next is to get rid of an old prejudice. Anonymous

Self-control is being disciplined

Every athlete in training
submits to strict discipline,
in order to be crowned with a wreath
that will not last; . . .
we do it for one that will last forever.
1 Corinthians 9:25

In his autobiography *Nigger,*
Dick Gregory, athlete and social activist,
tells how he disciplined his body
to run four hours each day,
even in the midst of winter.
He writes:
"I don't think I would ever have finished
high school without running.
I never got hungry while I was running,
even though we never ate breakfast at home
and I didn't always have enough money
for lunch. . . .
I was proud of my body . . .
and never had to take a rest."
Dick Gregory is a living example of what
Paul talks about in the Scripture reading.

How courageously
do I discipline my body and my spirit
to win a crown that will never perish?

What most people tend to forget
is that we have unbelievable control
over our destiny. Bill Gove

157

Journal

Self-control is suspending judgment

Jesus said, "Do not judge others, and God will not judge you." Luke 6:37

An employee opened a huge fiber glass container cluttering up the corner of a room in the Arkansas International Airport. In it was a batch of year-old, moldy mail. Someone had mistakenly moved it to the wrong spot. For a full year, 40,000 packages, letters, Christmas cards, bills, and invitations to the Inauguration of President Clinton lay unsent. Someone said, "Think of the sadness that mistake caused. Think of the people who felt slighted because they didn't get an expected Christmas gift! Think of Clinton's campaign contributors who felt betrayed because they didn't get an invitation to the inaugural. Think of the rash judgments people made by jumping to the wrong conclusion about why they didn't get an invitation or a gift."

How self-controlled am I when it comes to jumping to conclusions about people about whom I lack enough information to make a correct judgment?

When I look for the best in other people, I find the best in myself. Anonymous

Self-control is emulating Chi Chi

*I keep striving to win the prize
for which Christ Jesus
has already won me to himself. . . .
[I] forget what is behind me
and do my best to reach what is ahead.
So I run straight toward the goal
in order to win the prize.* Philippians 3:12–14

A professional golfer
who has won 24 PGA tournaments points
with pride to the fact that
he began his career driving balls
not at a New York country club
but in a Puerto Rican cane field,
driving oxen with a broomstick.
He says,
"I would walk behind an ox,
guiding him with a broomstick.
For $1 a day,
I worked eight hours straight,
with no food breaks."
That golfer was Chi Chi Rodriguez.

How willing am I
to work and make generous sacrifices
to spread God's kingdom?

*If you don't have a cause
that is worth dying for,
you very likely don't have anything
worth living for.* Author unknown

Other Books in this Series

JESUS: Meditations for the Millennium
GOD the FATHER: Meditations for the Millennium

Other Books by Mark Link

Bible 2000

Challenge 2000

Vision 2000

Mission 2000

Action 2000

For further information call or write:

Thomas More®
An RCL Company
200 East Bethany Drive
Allen, Texas 75002–3804

Toll Free   800–264–0368
Fax   800–688–8356

Daily Meditation Format

| *Begin each meditation with this prayer:* |

Father, you created me
and put me on earth for a purpose.
Jesus, you died for me
and called me to complete your work.
Holy Spirit, you help me
to carry out the work
for which I was created and called.
In your presence and name—
Father, Son, and Holy Spirit—
I begin my meditation.
May all my thoughts and inspirations
have their origin in you
and be directed to your glory.

| *Follow this format for each meditation:* |

1. READ the meditation prayerfully.
   (About one minute.)
2. THINK about what struck you most
   as you read the meditation. Why this?
   (About four minutes.)
3. SPEAK to God about your thoughts.
   (About one minute.)
4. LISTEN to God's response.
   Simply rest in God's presence
   with an open mind and an open heart.
   (About four minutes.)
5. END each meditation by praying the
   Lord's Prayer slowly and reverently.